YOUR CHINESE
HOROSCOPE FOR 1995

YOUR CHINESE HOROSCOPE FOR 1995

NEIL SOMERVILLE

What the Year of the Pig holds in store for you

Aquarian
An Imprint of HarperCollins*Publishers*

Aquarian
An Imprint of HarperCollins*Publishers*
77–85 Fulham Palace Road
Hammersmith, London W6 8JB
1160 Battery Street
San Francisco, California 94111–1213

Published by Aquarian 1994

10 9 8 7 6 5 4 3 2 1

A catalogue record for this book
is available from the British Library

ISBN 1 85538 386 1

Printed in Great Britain by
HarperCollinsManufacturing Glasgow

Illustrations by Josephine Sumner

CONTENTS

TO ROS, RICHARD AND EMILY.

INTRODUCTION

The origins of Chinese horoscopes have been lost in the mists of time. It is known that oriental astrologers practised their art many thousands of years ago and, even today, Chinese astrology continues to fascinate and intrigue.

In Chinese astrology there are 12 signs named after 12 different animals. No one quite knows how the signs acquired their names, but there is one legend that offers an explanation.

According to this legend, one Chinese New Year, the Buddha invited all the animals in his kingdom to come before him. Unfortunately – for reasons best known to the animals – only 12 turned up. The first to arrive was the Rat, followed by the Ox, Tiger, Rabbit, Dragon, Snake, Horse, Goat, Monkey, Rooster, Dog and finally the Pig.

In gratitude, the Buddha decided to name a year after each of the animals and those born during that year would inherit some of the personality of that animal. Therefore those born in the year of the Ox would be hard working, resolute and stubborn – just like the Ox – while those born in the year of the Dog would be loyal and faithful – just like the Dog.

While not everyone can possibly share all the characteristics of a sign, it is incredible what similarities do occur, and this is partly where the fascination of Chinese horoscopes lies.

In addition to the 12 signs of the Chinese zodiac there are also 5 elements and these have a strengthening or moderating influence upon the sign. Details about the effects of the elements are given in each of the chapters on the 12 signs.

To find out which sign you were born under, refer to the tables on pages ix-xii. As the Chinese year is based on the lunar year and does not start until late January or early February, it is particularly important for anyone born in those two months to check carefully the dates of the Chinese year in which they were born.

Also included, in the Appendix, are two charts showing the compatibility between the signs for both personal and business relationships, and details about the signs ruling the different hours of the day. From this it is possible to locate your ascendant and, as in Western astrology, this has a significant influence on your personality.

In writing this book, I have taken the unusual step of combining the intriguing nature of Chinese horoscopes with the Western desire to know what the future holds, and have based my interpretations upon various factors relating to each of the signs. This is the eighth year in which *Your Chinese Horoscope* has been published and I am pleased that so many have found the sections on the forthcoming year of benefit and that the advice has been constructive and helpful. Remember, though, that at all times you are the master of your own destiny. I sincerely hope that your Chinese horoscope for 1995 will prove interesting and helpful for the year ahead.

THE CHINESE YEARS

Rat	31 January	1900	to	18 February	1901
Ox	19 February	1901	to	7 February	1902
Tiger	8 February	1902	to	28 January	1903
Rabbit	29 January	1903	to	15 February	1904
Dragon	16 February	1904	to	3 February	1905
Snake	4 February	1905	to	24 January	1906
Horse	25 January	1906	to	12 February	1907
Goat	13 February	1907	to	1 February	1908
Monkey	2 February	1908	to	21 January	1909
Rooster	22 January	1909	to	9 February	1910
Dog	10 February	1910	to	29 January	1911
Pig	30 January	1911	to	17 February	1912
Rat	18 February	1912	to	5 February	1913
Ox	6 February	1913	to	25 January	1914
Tiger	26 January	1914	to	13 February	1915
Rabbit	14 February	1915	to	2 February	1916
Dragon	3 February	1916	to	22 January	1917
Snake	23 January	1917	to	10 February	1918
Horse	11 February	1918	to	31 January	1919
Goat	1 February	1919	to	19 February	1920
Monkey	20 February	1920	to	7 February	1921
Rooster	8 February	1921	to	27 January	1922
Dog	28 January	1922	to	15 February	1923
Pig	16 February	1923	to	4 February	1924

Rat	5 February	1924	to	24 January	1925
Ox	25 January	1925	to	12 February	1926
Tiger	13 February	1926	to	1 February	1927
Rabbit	2 February	1927	to	22 January	1928
Dragon	23 January	1928	to	9 February	1929
Snake	10 February	1929	to	29 January	1930
Horse	30 January	1930	to	16 February	1931
Goat	17 February	1931	to	5 February	1932
Monkey	6 February	1932	to	25 January	1933
Rooster	26 January	1933	to	13 February	1934
Dog	14 February	1934	to	3 February	1935
Pig	4 February	1935	to	23 January	1936
Rat	24 January	1936	to	10 February	1937
Ox	11 February	1937	to	30 January	1938
Tiger	31 January	1938	to	18 February	1939
Rabbit	19 February	1939	to	7 February	1940
Dragon	8 February	1940	to	26 January	1941
Snake	27 January	1941	to	14 February	1942
Horse	15 February	1942	to	4 February	1943
Goat	5 February	1943	to	24 January	1944
Monkey	25 January	1944	to	12 February	1945
Rooster	13 February	1945	to	1 February	1946
Dog	2 February	1946	to	21 January	1947
Pig	22 January	1947	to	9 February	1948
Rat	10 February	1948	to	28 January	1949
Ox	29 January	1949	to	16 February	1950
Tiger	17 February	1950	to	5 February	1951
Rabbit	6 February	1951	to	26 January	1952
Dragon	27 January	1952	to	13 February	1953
Snake	14 February	1953	to	2 February	1954
Horse	3 February	1954	to	23 January	1955

Goat	24 January	1955	to	11 February	1956
Monkey	12 February	1956	to	30 January	1957
Rooster	31 January	1957	to	17 February	1958
Dog	18 February	1958	to	7 February	1959
Pig	8 February	1959	to	27 January	1960
Rat	28 January	1960	to	14 February	1961
Ox	15 February	1961	to	4 February	1962
Tiger	5 February	1962	to	24 January	1963
Rabbit	25 January	1963	to	12 February	1964
Dragon	13 February	1964	to	1 February	1965
Snake	2 February	1965	to	20 January	1966
Horse	21 January	1966	to	8 February	1967
Goat	9 February	1967	to	29 January	1968
Monkey	30 January	1968	to	16 February	1969
Rooster	17 February	1969	to	5 February	1970
Dog	6 February	1970	to	26 January	1971
Pig	27 January	1971	to	14 February	1972
Rat	15 February	1972	to	2 February	1973
Ox	3 February	1973	to	22 January	1974
Tiger	23 January	1974	to	10 February	1975
Rabbit	11 February	1975	to	30 January	1976
Dragon	31 January	1976	to	17 February	1977
Snake	18 February	1977	to	6 February	1978
Horse	7 February	1978	to	27 January	1979
Goat	28 January	1979	to	15 February	1980
Monkey	16 February	1980	to	4 February	1981
Rooster	5 February	1981	to	24 January	1982
Dog	25 January	1982	to	12 February	1983
Pig	13 February	1983	to	1 February	1984
Rat	2 February	1984	to	19 February	1985
Ox	20 February	1985	to	8 February	1986

Tiger	9 February	1986	to	28 January	1987
Rabbit	29 January	1987	to	16 February	1988
Dragon	17 February	1988	to	5 February	1989
Snake	6 February	1989	to	26 January	1990
Horse	27 January	1990	to	14 February	1991
Goat	15 February	1991	to	3 February	1992
Monkey	4 February	1992	to	22 January	1993
Rooster	23 January	1993	to	9 February	1994
Dog	10 February	1994	to	30 January	1995
Pig	31 January	1995	to	18 February	1996

Note: The names of the signs in the Chinese zodiac occasionally differ in the various books on Chinese astrology, although the characteristics of the signs remain the same. In some books the Ox is referred to as the Buffalo or Bull, the Rabbit as the Hare or Cat, the Goat as the Sheep and the Pig as the Boar.

For the sake of convenience, the male gender is used throughout this book. Unless otherwise stated, the characteristics of the signs apply to both sexes.

Fortune turns like a wheel.
Chinese proverb.

WELCOME TO
THE YEAR OF THE PIG

Although the Pig may not be the most gainly of creatures, in Chinese horoscopes this sign is blessed with many virtues. The Pig is generally considered a genial, good-natured sign with a great capacity for enjoying itself and some of these traits will be evident in the Year of the Pig.

This will be a year which many will enjoy; it will be a positive year, a year of growth and one which holds many opportunities. There will be a prevailing sense of optimism, as many countries around the world enjoy a period of prosperity and expansion. Many industries will show signs of positive growth, consumer demand will be up and important agreements will be signed to stimulate international trade. In previous Pig years the Marshall Plan, the American sponsored European Recovery Programme, was inaugurated; EFTA, the European Free Trade Association, was formed and the United States took the significant step of lifting the 21-year embargo on trade with China. In the past, Pig years have favoured and encouraged commerce and 1995 will not be an exception. The upturn in activity is also likely to be reflected in the buoyant nature of the world stock markets and many will reach new highs over the year.

Politically, many governments will be more concerned with domestic than foreign policy and much attention will be given to legislation on welfare, help for the needy and improving health and public services. Many positive results are likely to come from the measures introduced. In previous Pig years, for instance, Nevada and Montana became the first states to introduce old age pensions and in Britain, the National Insurance Act helped lay the foundation of the modern welfare state.

There will also be major efforts to reduce the level of unemployment and while there will be some reduction due to the economic upturn, many governments will introduce new training schemes and take active measures to stimulate the employment markets.

Medical matters will also be given much prominence over the year and in addition to some pioneering operations there will also be some major breakthroughs in the treatment of certain diseases.

More ominously, previous Pig years have also seen significant uprisings and 1995 is unlikely to be an exception. Repressed nationalities and factions are likely to be active in focusing world attention on their causes and a spate of terrorist outrages could be committed over the year.

This year could also see some civil disturbances in certain African and Middle Eastern countries and in some cases governments and regimes will be overthrown. Developments in both Hong Kong and China are also likely to figure prominently in the news over the year and there could be some significant developments within the British Commonwealth.

However, while there will be some difficulties and tensions over the year, many worthy achievements will also take place. Individuals will reach new heights of endeavour and endurance and there will also be major steps forward in science and space discovery. It was in previous Pig years that Amundsen reached the South Pole, Thor Heyerdahl made his epic voyage on Kon-Tiki and, 12 years ago, Pioneer 10 became the first man-made object to travel beyond the solar system. This pattern of achievement will continue in 1995.

It is also likely that many world records will be broken over the year. These will not only be sporting and athletic records but also world speed records. Donald Campbell broke his world water speed record in Bluebird in a Pig year and among the records broken in the last Pig year was the world speed record for passenger trains, broken in France in September 1983. For those who follow sport or record-breaking events, 1995 could prove an exciting year!

Another characteristic of the Pig year is that it is often the time when distinctive fashions and trends emerge. The New Look female fashion became popular in a Pig year and so too did the dance the rumba. It is highly likely that other memorable and popular styles – some possibly quite daring! – will become the rage in 1995. The Pig is all for us having a good time and indeed many of us will have good cause to look back on the year with much satisfaction.

This will also be a year of personal opportunity. It is very much an action-orientated year and for those who are prepared to be bold and determined, it will prove particularly rewarding. Naturally some signs will fare better than others, but with optimism, enthusiasm and determination, almost all can benefit from the favourable trends that exist in the Year of the Pig. Generally, 1995 will be a year of achievement and I sincerely hope that the influence of the good-natured Pig will help to make this a good, positive and happy year for you.

31 JANUARY 1900 ~ 18 FEBRUARY 1901	*Metal Rat*
18 FEBRUARY 1912 ~ 5 FEBRUARY 1913	*Water Rat*
5 FEBRUARY 1924 ~ 24 JANUARY 1925	*Wood Rat*
24 JANUARY 1936 ~ 10 FEBRUARY 1937	*Fire Rat*
10 FEBRUARY 1948 ~ 28 JANUARY 1949	*Earth Rat*
28 JANUARY 1960 ~ 14 FEBRUARY 1961	*Metal Rat*
15 FEBRUARY 1972 ~ 2 FEBRUARY 1973	*Water Rat*
2 FEBRUARY 1984 ~ 19 FEBRUARY 1985	*Wood Rat*

THE
RAT

THE PERSONALITY OF THE RAT

The secret of success in life is for a man to be ready for his opportunity when it comes.

– Benjamin Disraeli: a Rat

The Rat is born under the sign of charm. He is intelligent, popular, and loves attending parties and large social gatherings. He is able to establish friendships with remarkable ease and people generally feel relaxed in his company. He is a very social creature and is genuinely interested in the welfare and activities of others. He has a good understanding of human nature and his advice and opinions are often sought.

The Rat is a hard and diligent worker. He is also very imaginative and is never short of ideas. However, he does sometimes lack the confidence to promote his ideas as much as he should and this can often prevent him from securing the recognition and credit he so often deserves.

The Rat is very observant and there are many who have made excellent writers and journalists. He also excels at personnel and PR work and any job which brings him into contact with people and the media. His skills are particularly appreciated in times of crisis, for the Rat has an incredibly strong sense of self-preservation. When it comes to finding a way out of an awkward situation, he is certain to be the one who comes up with a solution.

The Rat loves to be where there is a lot of action, but should he ever find himself in a very bureaucratic or restrictive environment he can become a stickler for discipline and routine.

He is also something of an opportunist and is constantly on the look-out for ways in which he can improve his wealth and lifestyle. He rarely lets an opportunity go by and can become involved in so many plans and schemes that he sometimes squanders his energies and achieves very little as a result. He is also rather gullible and can be taken in by those less scrupulous than himself.

Another characteristic of the Rat is his attitude to money. He is very thrifty and to some he may appear a little mean. The reason for this is purely that he likes to keep his money within his family. He can be most generous to his partner, his children, and close friends and relatives. He can also be generous to himself, for he often finds it impossible to deprive himself of any luxury or object which he fancies. The Rat is also very acquisitive and can be a notorious hoarder. He hates waste and is rarely prepared to throw anything away. He can also be rather greedy and will rarely refuse an invitation for a free meal or a complimentary ticket to some lavish function.

The Rat is a good conversationalist, although he can occasionally be a little indiscreet. He can be highly critical of others – for an honest and unbiased opinion, the Rat is a superb critic – and sometimes will use confidential information to his own advantage. However, as the Rat has such a bright and irresistible nature, most are prepared to forgive him for his slight indiscretions.

Throughout his long and eventful life, the Rat will make many friends and will find that he is especially well-suited to those born under his own sign and those of the Ox, Dragon and Monkey. The Rat can also get on well with those born under the signs of the Tiger, Snake, Rooster,

Dog and Pig, but the rather sensitive Rabbit and Goat will find the Rat a little too critical and blunt for their liking. The Horse and Rat will also find it difficult to get on with each other – the Rat craves security and will find the Horse's changeable moods and rather independent nature a little unsettling.

The Rat is very family orientated and will do anything to please his nearest and dearest. He is exceptionally loyal to his parents and can himself be a very caring and loving parent. He will take an interest in all his children's activities and will see that they want for nothing. The Rat usually has a large family.

The female Rat has a kindly, outgoing nature and involves herself in a multitude of different activities. She is a superb hostess and will usually have a wide circle of very good friends. She is conscientious about the upkeep of her home and has superb taste in home furnishings. She is extremely supportive to the other members of her family and, due to her resourceful, friendly and persevering nature, can do well in practically any career she enters.

Although the Rat is essentially outgoing and something of an extrovert, he is also a very private individual. He tends to keep his feelings to himself and, while he is not averse to learning what other people are doing, he resents anyone prying too closely into his own affairs. The Rat also does not like solitude and if he is alone for any length of time he can easily get depressed.

The Rat is undoubtedly very talented but more often than not he fails to capitalize on his many abilities. He has a tendency to become involved in too many schemes and chase after too many opportunities all at one time. If he were to slow down and concentrate on one thing at a time he could become very successful. If not, success and wealth could elude him. But the Rat, with his tremendous ability to charm, will rarely, if ever, be without friends.

THE FIVE DIFFERENT TYPES OF RAT

In addition to the 12 signs of the Chinese zodiac, there are five elements and these have a strengthening or moderating influence on the sign. The effects of the five elements on the Rat are described below, together with the years in which the elements were exercising their influence. Therefore all Rats born in 1900 and 1960 are Metal Rats, those born in 1912 and 1972 are Water Rats, and so on.

Metal Rat: 1900, 1960
This Rat has excellent taste and certainly knows how to appreciate the finer things in life. His home is comfortable and nicely decorated and he is forever entertaining or mixing in fashionable circles. He has considerable financial acumen and invests his money well. On the surface the Metal Rat appears cheerful and confident, but deep down he can be troubled by worries that are quite often of his own making. He is exceptionally loyal to his family and friends.

Water Rat: 1912, 1972

The Water Rat is intelligent and very astute. He is a deep thinker and can express his thoughts clearly and persuasively. He is always eager to learn and is talented in many different areas. The Water Rat is usually very popular but his fear of loneliness can sometimes lead him into mixing with the wrong sort of company. He is a particularly skilful writer, but he can get side-tracked very easily and should try to concentrate on just one thing at a time.

Wood Rat: 1924, 1984

The Wood Rat has a friendly, outgoing personality and is most popular with his colleagues and friends. He has a quick, agile brain and likes to turn his hand to anything he thinks may be useful. His one fear is insecurity, but given his intelligence and capabilities this fear is usually unfounded. He has a good sense of humour, enjoys travel and, due to his highly imaginative nature, can be a gifted writer or artist.

Fire Rat: 1936

The Fire Rat is rarely still and seems to have a never-ending supply of energy and enthusiasm. He loves being involved in the action – be it travel, following up new ideas, or campaigning for a cause in which he fervently believes. He is an original thinker and hates being bound by petty restrictions or the dictates of others. He can be forthright in his views, but can sometimes get carried away in the excitement of the moment and commit himself to various undertakings without checking what all the implications might be. He has a resilient nature and, with the right support, can often go far in life.

Earth Rat: 1948

This Rat is astute and very level-headed. He rarely takes unnecessary chances and, while he is constantly trying to improve his financial status, he is prepared to proceed slowly and leave nothing to chance. The Earth Rat is probably not as adventurous as the other types of Rat and prefers to remain in areas he knows rather than rush headlong into something he knows little about. He is talented, conscientious, and caring towards his loved ones, but at the same time can be self-conscious and worry a little too much about the image he is trying to project.

PROSPECTS FOR THE RAT IN 1995

The Chinese New Year starts on 31 January 1995. Until then, the old year, the Year of the Dog, is still making its presence felt. The Year of the Dog (10 February 1994 to 30 January 1995) will have been a reasonable year for the Rat, with the latter part of the year being a particularly constructive time for him. However, throughout the Dog year, the Rat will have found that he has obtained the best results by concentrating on areas that are familiar to him rather than experimenting with new ideas or embarking on anything too risky. If the Rat can keep this in mind and remain persistent in his various activities, he can end the year in a positive manner and with some pleasing gains to his credit.

The Rat is likely to do particularly well in his work at this time. There will be opportunities for him to make further progress and many Rats will be successful in obtaining a new position or be given more rewarding responsibilities. By pursuing any opportunities that he sees and remaining committed to his objectives, the Rat can make substantial progress. However, despite any success that he enjoys in his career, he cannot afford to be complacent in money matters. The Dog year is just not a time for him to take financial risks or to stretch his resources too far. If he does, he could experience some awkward problems later.

Another area that the Rat should watch is his relations with others. Although he is usually most considerate and enjoys good relations with those around him, he cannot afford to take the support of others for granted or be too demanding. To preserve good relations with others he needs to involve those around him in his various activities and also make sure that he devotes time to his loved ones. There is a danger that he could become too preoccupied with his own activities and, if he is not careful, strains and tensions could develop.

However, despite these words of caution, the closing months of the Dog year will be a generally rewarding and positive time for the Rat, with the period from November 1994 to January 1995 being a busy and productive time. The Rat could also receive some splendid personal news in December.

The Year of the Pig starts on 31 January 1995 and will be an interesting year for the Rat. Although not all the events that occur during the year will work out in his favour, with perseverance and the right attitude he will still be able to make pleasing progress in many areas of his life.

Socially, the year will be a busy and happy time for the Rat. He will be much in demand with his family and friends and can look forward to attending some enjoyable social events as well as widening his circle of friends. The year will prove particularly happy for the unattached Rat and romance is well aspected, especially in the spring and summer months. For any Rat who may have experienced some sadness in recent years or is feeling lonely, 1995 would be a good year to make every effort to start anew, to go out more and to build up a social life.

Anything positive that the Rat can do will be in his interests – but it is he, rather than others, who needs to make the initial effort.

The Rat's family is likely to give him much pleasure over the year and if he intends to start any major projects, such as carrying out improvements to his home, he would do well to enlist the help of others in his household rather than carrying out the work single-handed. Joint projects are likely to go particularly well and will give the Rat, and those around him, much satisfaction.

There could, however, be a domestic issue that arises over the year which does give cause for concern. Fortunately, it is unlikely to be serious, but the Rat should not hesitate to express his views on any matter that might be troubling him. To keep his thoughts to himself may only make matters worse and cause him additional anguish. Also, sometimes the Rat is prepared to fall in too readily with plans that he might have misgivings about and, again, this is something he does need to watch over the year.

The Rat can look forward to making steady progress in his work in 1995. However, this will not be possible without much effort on his part and he would do well to concentrate on specific objectives rather than spreading his energies too widely. There will be several opportunities for him to follow up over the year, especially in the spring, and many Rats can look forward to promotion or to obtaining a more interesting position as the year develops. However, the Rat needs to pay careful attention to the views of his colleagues and also make sure that he has the necessary support before proceeding with any of his ideas and plans. Should he meet with any opposition, he would do well to look at the reason why this is occurring and make any changes he feels necessary. By showing himself to be adaptable and conciliatory, the Rat will impress others and this will do much to enhance his future prospects. He should also give some thought to his future over the year and to what he would like to achieve in the next few years. If there are any training courses he can go on or any additional skills that he feels he needs, he would do well to follow these up. While 1995 will be a good year for him, 1996 will be even better and anything that he can do to enhance his future prospects will be very much to his advantage.

The Rat does, however, need to be careful in financial matters in 1995. Although he is usually astute when dealing with money matters, he can sometimes act impulsively or be overly indulgent. In 1995 he needs to be careful in *all* financial matters and would do well to check the small print of any important agreement he enters. He should also avoid committing his money to anything too speculative. This is not a year for taking financial risks.

Another area that the Rat needs to watch is his own well-being. Although he likes to keep himself active, sometimes he does not pay as much attention to himself as he should. He could be rushing his meals, not eating a balanced diet or putting himself under too much pressure. Over the year the Rat should make every effort to rectify any areas of neglect – and he will feel considerably better for doing so. In particular, he should try to make sure that he eats a well-balanced diet and, if he is in a stressful occupation, that he gives himself time to unwind properly. Some additional and regular exercise could prove especially beneficial for him.

On a personal level, 1995 will be quite a fulfilling year for the Rat. He will obtain much satisfaction from his various interests and if he has been thinking about taking up a new hobby or undertaking additional study, this would be an excellent year to do so. The Rat will also enjoy any travelling and holidays that he takes and he will find that outdoor activities such as gardening, walking or exploring the countryside will give him much pleasure. Indeed, anything that gives the Rat an opportunity to have a break from his usual daily routine would be in his best interests.

Generally, 1995 will be a pleasing year for the Rat and while not all his activities may work out as he anticipated, he will still do well. Socially and domestically, this will be a busy and happy year for him and, providing he is careful in money matters and takes good care of himself, he will enjoy the year. Anything that he can do to further his experience and skills will be well worth his while. This is, in many respects, a year of preparation for the better times that lie ahead for him in his own year, 1996, the Year of the Rat.

As far as the different types of Rat are concerned, 1995 will be a busy but enjoyable year for the *Metal Rat*. Over the year he will be much in demand with his family and friends, and domestically and socially this will be a generally pleasant year for him. A younger relation in particular is likely to be a great source of pride to him and any assistance that he feels he can give will be of great benefit. However, despite these generally favourable trends, he may have a rather awkward domestic problem to sort out. If such a situation does arise, he should not hesitate to seek the advice of those around him and of his many good friends. To try and sort out any awkward matter single-handed would not only put him under increased pressure but possibly prolong the problem unnecessarily. The Metal Rat will make steady progress in his work over the year and for those seeking employment or a new job, the spring and summer months are likely to be a favourable time for following up new opportunities. If he is able to obtain additional skills or widen his experience the Metal Rat will find that this will help him considerably in the next few years. He does, however, need to exercise caution in financial matters in 1995. Sometimes he can be rather extravagant in his spending and to stretch his resources too far could cause him some difficulty in the latter part of the year. The Metal Rat will, however, enjoy any travelling that he undertakes very much, especially if it is to areas new to him or ones that appeal to his adventurous nature. Also, in view of the generally demanding nature of the year, he would do well to make sure he sets some time aside to have a break from his usual daily activities. He could find a new hobby or interest especially beneficial, particularly if it gives him a chance to get out of doors or gives him some additional exercise.

This will be an interesting and varied year for the *Water Rat*. Socially and domestically, the year will contain many happy moments and, for the unattached Water Rat, the aspects for romance, for marriage and for making new friends are most encouraging. Indeed, all Water Rats will increase their circle of friends over the year and some of the contacts made will be most important in the future. The Water Rat can make steady progress in his work in 1995 and there will be opportunities for obtaining a new position or for widening his experience. However, he would do well to give some thought to his objectives over the year and to have some idea of what he wants to achieve. If not, he could miss some good opportunities and not make full use of his talents. He must also be realistic in his expectations. Sometimes the Water Rat tries to accomplish things before he has the necessary experience or without the proper preparation and this is something that he needs to guard against in 1995. In the words of Confucius, 'Desire to have things done quickly prevents their being done thoroughly.' If the Water Rat remembers this and sorts out his objectives and future aims, then he can make good progress and pave the way for future successes. The Water Rat also needs to exercise care in financial matters. Many Water Rats will be involved in large transactions over the year, maybe moving or buying a house, and the Water Rat does need to make sure he understands all the implications of any agreement that he enters. This is not a year in which he can take financial risks and, if he has any doubts, he would do well to seek professional advice. Those Water Rats involved in academic activities are likely to do well and it is also a favourable time for all Water Rats to obtain additional skills or qualifications. Those who are creatively inclined will get particular satisfaction from their interests and should try to promote their skills as much as they can. Generally, 1995 will be a constructive year for the Water Rat and his accomplishments over the year will go a long way towards contributing to his future successes.

This will be a pleasant year for the *Wood Rat*. He will have much time to devote to his hobbies and interests and these are likely to be a great source of satisfaction and enjoyment for him. They could also bring him into contact with those who share similar interests and many Wood Rats will make some new and important friendships as the year develops. The Wood Rat can also look forward to some enjoyable times with his family, although there could be times over the year when he feels others are making unreasonable demands on him. If this is the case, the Wood Rat should not hesitate to let others know his feelings and views. To be persuaded into doing something against his better judgement will only cause him much anguish and anxiety. He will find it best to be frank rather than suffer in silence. The Wood Rat will also be helped if he gives some thought to his future and to what he would like to accomplish in the next few years. Then, with some plan in mind, he can get down to achieving his objectives. The late summer can be a particularly positive time for him and one when he can start to put some of his longer term plans into motion, especially if they involve changing his accommodation. Although 1995 will contain moments of uncertainty and frustration, the Wood Rat will find that the events of the year will move in his favour, particularly in the second half of 1995. Travel is well aspected and the Wood Rat will very much enjoy any holiday or short breaks that he takes.

This will be an interesting year for the *Fire Rat*. Over the year several changes will take place which will have a significant bearing on his future. These changes could concern his work, his accommodation or personal situation and, although some could give him moments of anxiety, the Fire Rat will be able to turn the events of the year to his advantage. He is blessed with a resilient and determined nature and these qualities will serve him extremely well in 1995. Provided he is prepared to be adaptable and flexible in his outlook and sets about his various activities in a positive frame of mind, his achievements over the year can be considerable. In many ways the events of 1995 will help to sow the seeds for the progress he will make in the next few years. The Fire Rat should also listen carefully to the views of those around him. Although he may not agree with all he hears, both his family and colleagues speak with his interests at heart and he would do well to heed what they say. The Fire Rat's family, in particular, will be most supportive and if he feels in need of encouragement or advice, he should not hesitate to ask. Help and valuable assistance are there for the asking! The Fire Rat will derive much pleasure from his interests over the year, especially from any creative or outdoor interests that he might have, and also from any travelling that he undertakes. The closing months of the Year of the Pig will be especially busy time for him and it will be then and in 1996 that he will be able to enjoy the real rewards of his efforts.

The *Earth Rat* will enjoy 1995 and will be able to make pleasing progress in many of his activities. However, his degree of success is partly dependent on himself and his willingness to follow up any opportunities that he sees. Sometimes the Earth Rat tends to be rather cautious and guarded in his actions and this can often hold him back from achieving his full potential. In 1995 he should make a determined effort to go after his goals, whether personal or business, and his actions over the year will do much to help prepare him for the success he will enjoy in both this and the next few years. The spring and autumn months in particular are likely to be a rewarding time for him and it is then that he should remain alert for new positions and promotion opportunities. The Earth Rat can look forward to some very happy times with his family and friends and many will have good reason for a family celebration over the year. The Earth Rat should also make sure that he sets some regular time aside for his own interests, particularly if they enable him to have a break from his usual daily activities. To drive himself relentlessly without giving himself the opportunity to unwind and relax could leave him feeling tired and irritable and possibly prone to minor ailments. Like all Rats, the Earth Rat must be careful in financial matters over the year and avoid taking unnecessary risks with his money. He will, however, very much enjoy the travel that he undertakes in 1995 and a visit to some relations or friends he has not seen for some time could prove especially enjoyable.

FAMOUS RATS

Alan Alda, Dave Allen, Ursula Andress, Louis Armstrong, Charles Aznavour, Lauren Bacall, Shirley Bassey, Jeremy Beadle, Irving Berlin, Virginia Bottomley, Kenneth Branagh, Marlon Brando, Charlotte Brontë, Chris de Burgh, George Bush, Lord Callaghan, Jimmy Carter, Pablo Casals, Dick Cavett, Raymond Chandler, Maurice Chevalier, Linford Christie, Steve Cram, Barbara Dickson, Benjamin Disraeli, Noel Edmonds, T. S. Eliot, Ben Elton, Albert Finney, Clark Gable, Al Gore, Thomas Hardy, Vaclav Havel, Charlton Heston, Roy Hudd, Engelbert Humperdinck, Jeremy Irons, Glenda Jackson, Jean-Michel Jarre, Gene Kelly, F. W. de Klerk, Kris Kristofferson, Lawrence of Arabia, Gary Lineker, Andrew Lloyd Webber, Lulu, Henri Mancini, Earl Mountbatten, Robert Mugabe, Olivia Newton-John, Richard Nixon, Sean Penn, Enoch Powell, Prince, the Queen Mother, Vanessa Redgrave, Burt Reynolds, Jonathan Ross, Emma Samms, William Shakespeare, Wayne Sleep, Yves St Laurent, Tommy Steele, Shakin' Stevens, Donna Summer, James Taylor, Leo Tolstoy, the Prince of Wales, Dennis Waterman, Roger Whittaker, Kim Wilde, the Duke of York.

19 FEBRUARY 1901 ～ 7 FEBRUARY 1902   *Metal Ox*

6 FEBRUARY 1913 ～ 25 JANUARY 1914   *Water Ox*

25 JANUARY 1925 ～ 12 FEBRUARY 1926   *Wood Ox*

11 FEBRUARY 1937 ～ 30 JANUARY 1938   *Fire Ox*

29 JANUARY 1949 ～ 16 FEBRUARY 1950   *Earth Ox*

15 FEBRUARY 1961 ～ 4 FEBRUARY 1962   *Metal Ox*

3 FEBRUARY 1973 ～ 22 JANUARY 1974   *Water Ox*

20 FEBRUARY 1985 ～ 8 FEBRUARY 1986   *Wood Ox*

THE
OX

THE PERSONALITY OF THE OX

What you ardently and constantly desire, you always get.
— Napoleon Bonaparte: an Ox

The Ox is born under the signs of equilibrium and tenacity. He is a hard and conscientious worker and sets about everything he does in a resolute, methodical and determined manner. He has considerable leadership qualities and is often admired for his tough and uncompromising nature. He knows what he wants to achieve in life and, as far as possible, will not be deflected from his ultimate objective.

The Ox takes his responsibilities and duties very seriously. He is decisive and quick to take advantage of any opportunity that comes his way. He is also sincere and places a great deal of trust in his friends and colleagues. He is, nevertheless, something of a loner. He is a quiet and private individual and often keeps his thoughts to himself. He also cherishes his independence and prefers to set about things in his own way rather than be bound by the dictates of others or be influenced by outside pressures.

The Ox tends to have a calm and tranquil nature, but if something angers him or he feels that someone has let him down, he can have a fearsome temper. He can also be stubborn and obstinate and this can lead him into conflict with others. Usually the Ox will succeed in getting his own way, but should things go against him, he is a poor loser and will take any defeat or set-back extremely badly.

The Ox is often a deep thinker and rather studious. He is not particularly renowned for his sense of humour and does not take kindly to new gimmicks or anything too innovative. The Ox is too solid and traditional for that and he prefers to stick to the more conventional norm.

His home is very important to him and in some respects he treats it as a private sanctuary. His family tends to be closely knit and the Ox will make sure that each member does their fair share around the house. The Ox tends to be a hoarder, but he is always well-organized and neat. He also places great importance on punctuality and there is nothing that infuriates him more than to be kept waiting – particularly if it is due to someone's inefficiency. The Ox can be a hard taskmaster!

Once settled in a job or house the Ox will quite happily remain there for many years. He does not like change and he is also not particularly keen on travel. He does, however, enjoy gardening and other outdoor pursuits and he will often spend much of his spare time out of doors. The Ox is usually an excellent gardener and whenever possible he will always make sure he has a large area of ground to maintain. The Ox usually prefers to live in the country rather than the town.

Due to his dedicated and dependable nature, he will usually do well in his chosen career, providing he is given enough freedom to act on his own initiative. He invariably does well in politics, agriculture and in careers which need specialized training. The Ox is also very gifted in the arts and there are many who have enjoyed considerable success as musicians or composers.

The Ox is not as outgoing as some and it often takes him a long time to establish friendships and feel relaxed in another person's company. His courtships are likely to be long, but once he is settled he will remain devoted and loyal to his partner. The Ox is particularly well-suited to those born under the signs of the Rat, Rabbit, Snake and Rooster. He can also establish a good relationship with the Monkey, Dog, Pig and another Ox, but he will find that he has little in common with the whimsical and sensitive Goat. He will also find it difficult to get on with the Horse, Dragon and Tiger – the Ox prefers a quiet and peaceful existence and those born under these three signs tend to be a little too lively and impulsive for his liking.

The lady Ox has a kind and caring nature, and her home and family are very much her pride and joy. She always tries to do her best for her partner and can be a most conscientious and loving parent. The lady Ox is an excellent organizer and she is also a very determined person who will often succeed in getting what she wants in life. She usually has a deep interest in the arts and is often a talented artist or musician.

The Ox is a very down-to-earth character. He is sincere, loyal and unpretentious. He can, however, be rather reserved and to some he may appear distant and aloof. He has a quiet nature, but underneath he is very strong-willed and ambitious. He has the courage of his convictions and is often prepared to stand up for what he believes is right, regardless of the consequences. He inspires confidence and trust and throughout his life he will rarely be short of people who are ready to support him or who admire his strong and resolute manner.

THE FIVE DIFFERENT TYPES OF OX

In addition to the 12 signs of the Chinese zodiac, there are five elements and these have a strengthening or moderating influence on the sign. The effects of the five elements on the Ox are described below, together with the years in which the elements were exercising their influence. Therefore all Oxen born in 1901 and 1961 are Metal Oxen, those born in 1913 and 1973 are Water Oxen, and so on.

Metal Ox: 1901, 1961
This Ox is confident and very strong-willed. He can be blunt and forthright in his views and is not afraid of speaking his mind. He sets about his objectives with a dogged determination, but he can become so wrapped up in his various activities that he can be oblivious to the thoughts and feelings of those around him, and this can sometimes be to his detriment. He is honest and dependable and will never promise more than he can deliver. He has a good appreciation of the arts and usually has a small circle of very good and loyal friends.

Water Ox: 1913, 1973
This Ox has a sharp and penetrating mind. He is a good organizer and sets about his work in a methodical manner. He is not as narrow-minded as some of the other types of Oxen and is more willing to involve others in his plans and aspirations. He usually has very high moral standards and is often attracted to careers in public service. He is a good

judge of character and has such a friendly and persuasive manner that he usually experiences little difficulty in securing his objectives. He is popular and has an excellent way with children.

Wood Ox: 1925, 1985

The Wood Ox conducts himself with an air of dignity and authority and will often take a leading role in any enterprise in which he gets involved. He is very self-confident and is direct in his dealings with others. He does, however, have a quick temper and has no hesitation in speaking his mind. He has tremendous drive and will-power and has an extremely good memory. The Wood Ox is particularly loyal and devoted to the members of his family and has a most caring nature.

Fire Ox: 1937

The Fire Ox has a powerful and assertive personality and is a hard and conscientious worker. He holds strong views and has very little patience when things do not go his own way. He can also get carried away in the excitement of the moment and does not always take into account the views of those around him. He nevertheless has many leadership qualities and will often reach positions of power, eminence and wealth. He usually has a small group of loyal and close friends and is very devoted to his family.

Earth Ox: 1949

This Ox sets about everything he does in a sensible and level-headed manner. He is ambitious, but he is also realistic in his aims and is often prepared to work long hours in order to secure his objectives. He is shrewd in financial and business matters and is a very good judge of character. He has a quiet nature and is greatly admired for his sincerity and integrity. He is also very loyal to his family and friends and his views and opinions are often sought by others.

PROSPECTS FOR THE OX IN 1995

The Chinese New Year starts on 31 January 1995. Until then, the old year, the Year of the Dog, is still making its presence felt. The Year of the Dog (10 February 1994 to 30 January 1995) will have been a variable year for the Ox and he may have experienced problems and delays in several areas of his life. However, the Ox is blessed with a robust and resilient nature and although the Dog year may have been frustrating at times, he can still make progress and even turn set-backs to his advantage. Indeed, the second half of the Dog year is a much more favourable time for him and all Oxen will see a gradual upturn in their fortunes.

For what remains of the Dog year, the Ox should continue to set about his work in his usual determined and conscientious manner. If, however, he meets with any opposition from others, particularly work colleagues, he should seek compromise rather than confrontation. To impair relations unnecessarily could leave him lacking support when he may need it later. Likewise, those Oxen seeking employment should pursue any opportunities that they see. Admittedly some Oxen will have had a difficult time in the Dog year but, as the proverb goes, every cloud has a silver lining, and that silver lining is gradually appearing. Anything constructive that the Ox can do in work matters will be very much to his advantage and he could reap substantial results from his efforts in the new year.

The Ox's social and domestic life is, however, likely to be very busy at this time and his family and friends will be a great source of pleasure to him. For those Oxen who are unattached or who may have been feeling lonely, the prospects for romance and for making friends are most encouraging and this positive trend will continue through to the Year of the Pig as well. Socially, November and December will be two active and enjoyable months.

If the Ox has any spare time in the closing stages of the Dog year, he should give some thought to what he would like to accomplish in the next 12 months. He would also do well to discuss his ideas with others. The Year of the Pig will be a year of considerable opportunity for the Ox and by having some idea of what he would like to do he will be better placed to take advantage of the opportunities that it will bring.

The Year of the Pig starts on 31 January and is going to be a busy and constructive year for the Ox. He will do well in most of his activities, although his level of success is partly dependent upon his degree of commitment and his also having a clear idea of his objectives. For the deter-

mined Ox – and most Oxen do have a determined nature!
– the rewards of the year can be quite considerable.

Over the year there will be several opportunities for the
Ox to pursue in his work and many Oxen will be
successful in obtaining a new job, being promoted or being
given more rewarding responsibilities. Throughout 1995
the Ox should follow up any opportunities that he sees and
make every effort to promote his skills and ideas.

Although the Ox can sometimes be a loner and likes to
retain a certain independence in his actions, the year does
favour joint endeavours and he would do well to involve
others in his plans and activities. His colleagues will be
generally supportive and willing to help him and the Ox
should not hesitate to avail himself of this help. Despite his
will-power and tenacity, even he cannot achieve everything
single-handed! Also, if he is able to add to his skills and
experience over the year, he will find that this will serve
him well in the future.

Those Oxen seeking work should again follow up any
openings that they see and also investigate any training
courses they might be eligible for. It may also be in their
interests to consider types of work they have not undertaken before. The challenge this would give could prove
particularly stimulating for the Ox as well as opening up a
number of opportunities for the future. The spring and
summer months will be a particularly good time for
employment opportunities.

Although the Ox may not consider himself to be a great
socializer, the social events that he attends over the year
will prove most enjoyable. He will also build up some new
friendships and contacts as the year develops; several of

these will prove most important to him in the next few years. For the Ox who is young and free, 1995 will contain many happy and memorable moments!

While the Ox's social life will go well, he may have to deal with a few domestic problems. These could concern a misunderstanding with a relation and, in such a situation, the Ox would do well to try and sort the matter out as it arises rather than allow it to continue, possibly escalate and mar what will otherwise be a constructive year for him. Alternatively, the Ox may have to help a loved one overcome a problem. At the time this could put some additional strain on him, but he can take comfort from the knowledge that any support and advice he can give will do much good and be valued more than he may realize at the time. Others often regard the Ox as a tower of strength in difficult times and his calmness and common sense are greatly appreciated.

The Ox would also do well to involve his family in his various activities over the year. Sometimes, usually quite unintentionally, he can get so absorbed in his own activities that he does not always pay as much attention to what is going on around him as he should. To preserve domestic harmony, he would do well to set some time aside for those around him and make sure he involves himself in their interests.

The Ox will do well in financial matters over the year and is likely to end the year in a more secure financial position than he was in at the start. He could also be quite successful in purchases he makes, particularly for himself and his home, and by looking around he could acquire several excellent bargains. While he cannot afford to take undue risks with his money, some investments he makes could prove most successful.

Although the Ox may not travel as far in 1995 as he has done in recent years, the travelling he does undertake will go well. He should ensure that he has at least one good break over the year and if he is able to take a holiday over the summer months he is likely to find this particularly enjoyable and beneficial for him.

Generally, 1995 will be a pleasing year for the Ox. By setting about his activities in his usual diligent way and by acting in conjunction with others, he can make considerable progress. There will also be some excellent opportunities to pursue, particularly in his career, and with a determined outlook he can go a long way towards improving his present position. He can also look forward to making some good friends over the year, although it would be in his interests to handle domestic matters with care and forethought.

As far as the different types of Ox are concerned, 1995 will be a satisfying year for the *Metal Ox*. He is blessed with a most determined nature and usually knows what he wants in life, and these two qualities will serve him well over the year. By setting about his various activities in his usual determined manner, he will be able to make considerable progress, especially in his work. There will be several excellent opportunities for him to pursue, particularly in the spring, and those Metal Oxen seeking work should actively pursue any openings that might be available to them. It will also help the Metal Ox to try to extend his skills over the year and any additional experience he can gain will serve him well in the future. He will be successful in financial matters in 1995 and while he would still do well to avoid any risky undertakings, he will see a substantial improvement in his financial situation and could be fortunate in some purchases and investments. The Metal Ox will also devote considerable time to family matters in 1995 and a younger relation is likely to be a great source of pride to him. He will find those around him most supportive and if he feels under pressure or has any problems that are concerning him, he should not hesitate to let others know. Not only will keeping problems to himself increase his burden, but he will also find that others can give him much useful advice and assistance. Socially, this will also be an active year and the Metal Ox is likely to extend his circle of contacts and friends quite considerably. Any Metal Oxen who are unattached or who feel that they need another interest should make every effort to go out more and possibly join a local club or society. This will bring them into contact with others as well as giving them an additional interest and new source of enjoyment. All Metal Oxen will find that by taking positive action, no matter what area of life it may concern, they can turn this into a successful, profitable and enjoyable year.

This will be a significant year for the *Water Ox*. Over the course of the year several events will occur that will cause him to adjust and reconsider some of his plans. Although at the time this may cause the Water Ox some anxiety, the long-term consequences of the decisions and actions that he takes will work out well and in the future he could come to view some of what happens in 1995 as 'blessings in disguise'. Throughout the year the Water Ox should continue to set about his activities in his usual methodical manner, but when obstacles or new situations arise, he should be prepared to be flexible and consider all the options available to him. By acting in this way he may not only improve and strengthen his original ideas and plans, but will win the support and respect of others. This is a year of numerous possibilities and much of what occurs will help guide, direct and prepare him for his future success. The Water Ox will also be much in demand with his family and friends and socially this will be a busy and eventful year. Although his family and those close to him will give him much happiness, he may still have an awkward domestic matter to deal with. Fortunately this is likely to be short-lived, but he will find it better to speak openly about any matter causing him concern rather than letting it simmer in the background. He will in any case find that his considerate and thoughtful nature will do much to ease any problems that arise. He will be fortunate in financial matters in 1995, but should try not to stretch his resources too far or enter into any commitment without checking whether he can meet the obligations that he may be placed under. Generally, 1995 will be a constructive and enjoyable year for the Water Ox and provided he is prepared to be flexible in his outlook, his achievements and the plans that he makes over the year will help to sow the seeds of his future progress and success.

This will be a satisfying year for the *Wood Ox*. He will obtain considerable pleasure over the year from his various hobbies and interests and, if he is able, he would do well to consider taking up a new interest, possibly something unrelated to anything he has done before. He will find this both stimulating and challenging and could even discover skills he did not know he possessed! By using any spare time he has constructively, he will have many enjoyable and satisfying moments over the year. The Wood Ox can also look forward to being in demand with his family and friends. While, like all Oxen, he will need to deal with domestic matters with care and understanding, his family and social life will generally go well and give him much happiness. Any Wood Ox who may have felt lonely in recent years should make every effort to go out more and also consider joining a local club or getting in contact with those who share his interests. By making the effort he will be able to build up some new and valuable friendships. He is also likely to carry out alterations to his home and garden over the year and while he will be pleased with the finished result, he should be wary of taking risks with dangerous pieces of equipment or lifting particularly heavy objects. A strain or minor accident could cause him some unnecessary suffering and throughout the year the Wood Ox does need to be careful when undertaking any DIY or energetic activities. He will, however, be quite successful in financial matters and many Wood Oxen can look forward to receiving an additional and unexpected sum of money during the year. The Wood Ox should also enter any competitions that catch his eye – 1995 will hold several pleasant surprises for him and winning a prize could be one of them!

This will be a satisfying year for the *Fire Ox* and he will be able to make progress in many of his activities. However, it would help him to have an idea of what he would like to achieve, both in this and in the next few years. He can then work purposefully towards achieving his aims as well as following up any opportunities that he sees. This is a year in which he can achieve worthwhile results in many of his endeavours, but to make the most of the positive trends that exist he does need to think about his future and to plan rather than leave everything to chance. He will find his family and colleagues are most supportive and he would do well to seek their views on his ideas or on any matters that may be giving him concern. The Fire Ox will find that he will make greater progress over the year if he involves others in his various activities rather than taking on too much single-handed. He can also look forward to leading an enjoyable social life over the year and many Fire Oxen will have good cause for a personal celebration. April and May in particular could prove significant months. The Fire Ox will be generally successful in financial matters in 1995, although he would do well to exercise care if he enters into any particularly large transaction or has to complete any important forms. An oversight could take some time to sort out. In spite of the many demands on him, he should also ensure that he sets some time aside for his own interests and gives himself the chance to unwind from everyday pressures. He will find outdoor activities, particularly those that give him some additional exercise, especially beneficial. This year will contain many enjoyable and satisfying moments for him and by planning and arranging his activities well he can turn it into a highly successful and rewarding one.

This will be a busy year for the *Earth Ox* and while he will make worthwhile progress, several changes will take place which could effect his plans and future objectives.

These changes could take place in almost any sphere of his life, from his work to his personal situation, and while they may give the Earth Ox moments of anxiety he will emerge from the year in a much improved situation. He will find that out of change will come new and brighter opportunities – opportunities that might not have been available to him before. The events that happen over the year will also enable the Earth Ox to consider and review his present situation, and by doing so, he will be able to develop new ideas and plans. By being positive in the face of change and by continuing to set about his activities in his usual conscientious manner, the Earth Ox can turn 1995 into a very constructive and significant year. If he is able to add to his skills and gain additional experience in a new area he will also find that this will do much to enhance his future prospects. The Earth Ox will lead a pleasant domestic and social life over the year and can look forward to attending several most enjoyable social functions. Some people he meets at one of these functions will prove most important to him in the future. All Earth Oxen will find that their circle of friends and acquaintances will increase substantially over the year. The Earth Ox does, however, need to deal with domestic matters with care and pay due attention to the views and feelings of those around him. To preserve domestic harmony he should also try to involve those around him in his various interests and encourage joint family activities. Generally, despite the busy and demanding nature of the year, the Earth Ox will enjoy much of 1995 and emerge with many gains to his credit.

FAMOUS OXEN

Hans Christian Andersen, Johann Sebastian Bach, Warren Beatty, Tony Benn, Jon Bon Jovi, Rory Bremner, Jeff Bridges, Benjamin Britten, Frank Bruno, Richard Burton, Barbara Bush, Johnny Carson, Barbara Cartland, Judith Chalmers, Charlie Chaplin, Warren Christopher, George Cole, Natalie Cole, Peter Cook, Bill Cosby, Tom Courtenay, Tony Curtis, Sammy Davis Jr, Jacques Delors, Walt Disney, Patrick Duffy, Harry Enfield, Jane Fonda, Michael Foot, Gerald Ford, Edward Fox, Michael J. Fox, George Frederick Handel, King Harold V of Norway, Robert Hardy, Nigel Havers, Adolf Hitler, Dustin Hoffman, Anthony Hopkins, Billy Joel, Don Johnson, Jack Jones, King Juan Carlos of Spain, B. B. King, Mark Knopfler, Burt Lancaster, Jessica Lange, Angela Lansbury, Jack Lemmon, Nicholas Lyndhurst, John MacGregor, David Mellor, Warren Mitchell, Eddie Murphy, Napoleon, Jawaharlal Nehru, Paul Newman, Jack Nicholson, Oscar Peterson, Colin Powell, Robert Redford, Peter Paul Rubens, Willie Rushton, Arthur Scargill, Monica Seles, Peter Sellers, Jean Sibelius, Valerie Singleton, Jimmy Somerville, Sissy Spacek, Bruce Springsteen, Rod Steiger, Meryl Streep, Loretta Swit, Lady Thatcher, Twiggy, Mary Tyler Moore, Dick Van Dyke, the Princess of Wales, Zoë Wanamaker, the Duke of Wellington, Alan Whicker, Ernie Wise, W. B. Yeats.

8 FEBRUARY 1902 ～ 28 JANUARY 1903 *Water Tiger*

26 JANUARY 1914 ～ 13 FEBRUARY 1915 *Wood Tiger*

13 FEBRUARY 1926 ～ 1 FEBRUARY 1927 *Fire Tiger*

31 JANUARY 1938 ～ 18 FEBRUARY 1939 *Earth Tiger*

17 FEBRUARY 1950 ～ 5 FEBRUARY 1951 *Metal Tiger*

5 FEBRUARY 1962 ～ 24 JANUARY 1963 *Water Tiger*

23 JANUARY 1974 ～ 10 FEBRUARY 1975 *Wood Tiger*

9 FEBRUARY 1986 ～ 28 JANUARY 1987 *Fire Tiger*

THE
TIGER

THE PERSONALITY OF THE TIGER

Success is a science. If you have the conditions, you get the result.

— Oscar Wilde: a Tiger

The Tiger is born under the sign of courage. He is a charismatic figure and usually holds very firm views and beliefs. He is strong-willed and determined, and sets about most of the things he does with a tremendous energy and enthusiasm. He is very alert and quick-witted and his mind is forever active. He is a highly original thinker and is nearly always brimming with new ideas or full of enthusiasm for some new project or scheme.

The Tiger adores challenges and he loves to get involved in anything which he thinks has an exciting future or which catches his imagination. He is prepared to take risks and does not like to be bound either by convention or the dictates of others. The Tiger likes to be free to act as he chooses and at least once during his life he will throw caution to the wind and go off and do the things he wants to do.

The Tiger does, however, have a somewhat restless nature. Even though he is often prepared to throw himself wholeheartedly into a project, his initial enthusiasm can soon wane if he sees something more appealing. He can also be rather impulsive and there will have been occasions in his life when he has acted in a manner which he has later regretted. If the Tiger were to think things out or to persevere in his various activities, he would almost certainly enjoy a greater degree of success.

Fortunately the Tiger is lucky in most of his enterprises, but should things not work out as he had hoped, he is liable to suffer from severe bouts of depression and it will often take him a long time to recover. The Tiger's life often consists of a series of ups and downs.

The Tiger is, however, very adaptable. He has an adventurous spirit and rarely stays in the same place for long. In the early stages of his life he is likely to try his hand at several different jobs and he will also change his residence fairly frequently.

The Tiger is very honest and open in his dealings with others. He hates any sort of hypocrisy or falsehood. He is also well known for being blunt and forthright and has no hesitation in speaking his mind. He can also be most rebellious at times, particularly against any form of petty authority, and while this can lead the Tiger into conflict with others, he is never one to shrink from an argument or avoid standing up for what he believes is right.

The Tiger is a natural leader and can invariably rise to the top of his chosen profession. He does not, however, care for anything too bureaucratic or detailed and he also does not like to obey orders. He can be stubborn and obstinate and throughout his life he likes to retain a certain amount of independence in his actions and be responsible to no one but himself. He likes to consider that all his achievements are due to his own efforts and unless he cannot avoid it, he will rarely ask for support from others.

Ironically, despite his self-confidence and leadership qualities, the Tiger can be indecisive and will often delay making a major decision until the very last moment. He can also be sensitive to criticism.

Although the Tiger is capable of earning large sums of money, he is rather a spendthrift and does not always put his money to its best use. He can also be most generous and will often shower lavish gifts on friends and relations.

The Tiger cares very much for his reputation and the image that he tries to project. He carries himself with an air of dignity and authority and enjoys being the centre of attention. He is very adept at attracting publicity, both for himself and for the causes he supports.

The Tiger often marries young and he will find himself best suited to those born under the signs of the Pig, Dog, Horse and Goat. He can also get on well with the Rat, Rabbit and Rooster, but will find the Ox and Snake a bit too quiet and too serious for his liking, and he will also be highly irritated by the Monkey's rather mischievous and inquisitive ways. The Tiger will also find it difficult to get on with another Tiger or a Dragon – both partners will want to dominate the relationship and could find it difficult to compromise on even the smallest of matters.

The Tigress is lively, witty and a marvellous hostess at parties. She is usually most attractive and takes great care over her appearance. She can also be a very doting mother and while she believes in letting her children have their freedom, she makes an excellent teacher and will ensure that her children are brought up well and want for nothing. Like her male counterpart, she has numerous interests and likes to have sufficient independence and freedom to go off and do the things that she wants to do. She also has a most caring and generous nature.

The Tiger has many commendable qualities. He is honest, courageous and often a source of inspiration for others. Providing he can curb the wilder excesses of his restless nature, he is almost certain to lead a most fulfilling and satisfying life.

THE FIVE DIFFERENT TYPES
OF TIGER

In addition to the 12 signs of the Chinese zodiac, there are five elements and these have a strengthening or moderating influence on the sign. The effects of the five elements on the Tiger are described below, together with the years in which the elements were exercising their influence. Therefore all Tigers born in 1950 are Metal Tigers, those born in 1902 and 1962 are Water Tigers and so on.

Metal Tiger: 1950
The Metal Tiger has an assertive and outgoing personality. He is very ambitious and, while his aims may change from time to time, he will work relentlessly until he has obtained what he wants. He can, however, be impatient for results and also get highly strung if things do not work out as he would like. He is distinctive in his appearance and is admired and respected by many.

Water Tiger: 1902, 1962
This Tiger has a wide variety of interests and is always eager to experiment with new ideas or go off and explore distant lands. He is versatile, shrewd and has a kindly

nature. The Water Tiger tends to remain calm in a crisis, although he can be annoyingly indecisive at times. He communicates well with others and through his many capabilities and persuasive nature he usually achieves what he wants in life. He is also highly imaginative and is often a gifted orator or writer.

Wood Tiger: 1914, 1974

The Wood Tiger has a very friendly and pleasant personality. He is less independent than some of the other types of Tiger and is more prepared to work with others to secure a desired objective. However, he does have a tendency to jump from one thing to another and can get easily distracted. He is usually very popular, has a large circle of friends and invariably leads a busy and enjoyable social life. He also has a good sense of humour.

Fire Tiger: 1926, 1986

The Fire Tiger sets about everything he does with great verve and enthusiasm. He loves action and is always ready to throw himself wholeheartedly into anything which catches his imagination. He has many leadership qualities and is capable of communicating his ideas and enthusiasm to others. He is very much an optimist and can be most generous. He has a likeable nature and can be a witty and persuasive speaker.

Earth Tiger: 1938

This Tiger is responsible and level-headed. He studies everything objectively and tries to be scrupulously fair in all his dealings. Unlike other Tigers, he is prepared to specialize in certain areas rather than get distracted by other matters, but he can become so involved with what he is doing that he does not always take into account the views and opinions of those around him. He has good business sense and is usually very successful in later life. He has a large circle of friends and pays great attention to both his appearance and his reputation.

PROSPECTS FOR THE TIGER IN 1995

The Chinese New Year starts on 31 January 1995. Until then, the old year, the Year of the Dog, is still making its presence felt. The Year of the Dog (10 February 1994 to 30 January 1995) will have been a busy year for the Tiger and he is likely to have made progress in many of his activities. However, as he will have found, to achieve anything in the Dog year will have required much effort and persistence on his part. This still applies to the closing stages of the year.

For what remains of the Year of the Dog, the Tiger should remain committed to his plans and continue to set about his activities in his usual determined way. He would also do well to concentrate on specific matters rather than try to do too much all at the same time. If he wishes to make progress in his work, then this is where he should concentrate his efforts or, if he intends to undertake some home improvements or carry out some other objective, he should concentrate on this. To spread his energies too widely will not only lessen the amount he achieves but also leave him feeling exhausted. The Year of the Dog is a time for sorting out his priorities and concentrating on these.

The Tiger can, however, look forward to having some splendid times with his family and friends in the closing months of the year. He can also expect some pleasing personal news in December or early January, and it would be in his interests to pay careful attention to all that is going on around him at this time.

There is also a likelihood that he will go on several long journeys towards the end of the year and the travelling he undertakes will prove most enjoyable and interesting. If he is able to rest and unwind during any break away he will find this most beneficial for him, particularly in view of the demanding nature of the Dog year.

The Tiger will also be generally fortunate in financial matters although in the last two months of the year he would do well to keep a watch over his outgoings. He could find that his expenditure is more than he has budgeted for and without care this could lead to problems later.

Generally, however, the Year of the Dog is a positive time for the Tiger and by making the most of his abilities and concentrating his efforts on specific objectives, he can accomplish much in the closing stages of the year.

The Year of the Pig begins on 31 January and as it favours innovation and enterprise, two qualities very strong in the Tiger, he is likely to thrive throughout the year and can look forward to making considerable progress in many areas of his life.

One area which is especially well aspected for the Tiger is his work. If he is seeking employment, promotion or a new position, he should pursue any opportunities that he sees and, even if at the first attempt, he is not successful, he should persist until he has got what he wants. Throughout the year the Tiger will find that progress, results and rewards are his if he persists long enough. He should also advance any ideas and plans that he has and, even if one or two may not work out as he hopes, he should not give up. Over the year the Tiger will find much truth in the saying, 'Nothing ventured, nothing gained.' For the determined and enterprising Tiger, progress and achievement in the Year of the Pig can be considerable.

The Tiger does, however, need to exercise care in financial matters. He should not get involved in any risky or speculative ventures – or at least not until he has checked all the facts carefully. He would also do well to keep a watch over his level of expenditure. Sometimes he can be a little too extravagant and indulgent with his spending and without care he could find that his outgoings are considerably more than he anticipated. He also needs to exercise great care if he gets involved in any legal matter over the year and, if he does, he would do well to obtain professional advice. Fortunately these words of warning only apply to a few Tigers, but legal matters could cause problems for the Tiger in 1995 and it is an area which he does need to watch closely.

On a more positive note, the Tiger can look forward to leading a pleasing social life over the year. For the unattached Tiger there will be plenty of opportunities to make new friends although it would be in his interests to let any new romance build up gradually rather than rush into any commitment. April, May and September are likely to be particularly happy and memorable months for the single Tiger.

Domestically, the Tiger's family will also be a great source of pleasure to him. They will give him much valuable support in his various activities and the Tiger would do well to listen to any advice that they offer him. He will also find some of his ideas and plans strengthened if he involves others rather than just relying on his own efforts. The Tiger also needs to ensure that he sets time aside to devote to his loved ones and their interests. In view of the busy nature of the year, it would be all too easy for the Tiger to get so emersed in his own concerns that he does not devote as much time to others as he should and this could result in problems and tensions.

The Tiger is likely to carry out a number of improvements to his home and garden over the year and, while this may take longer than he anticipated, he will be delighted with the finished result. Again, if he is able to share this work with the other members of his household, he will find that the results he obtains will be that much more satisfying and, indeed, quicker. For domestic enterprises, concerted efforts will bring the best results, even though the Tiger does like to do a lot on his own!

If the Tiger intends to move over the year, he could find a new home ideal for his needs and while the actual process of moving will involve him in much time and effort, he will be pleased with how it works out. He could find a change of area will lead to new opportunities and new friends. However, as with all major transactions over the year, the Tiger does need to make sure all the paperwork concerning any move is in order and that he is aware of all the implications.

There will also be several opportunities for the Tiger to indulge in his love of travel over the year, sometimes at short notice. However, in all his travels, he does need to ensure that his connections and itinerary are worked out beforehand. Without such planning he could find some of the journeys he undertakes are not as smooth as he would have liked! If he is visiting an area new to him, it would also be worth his while to learn something about it before he leaves. If not, he could find he is ill-equipped and ill-prepared and will not have such a good time away as he otherwise might.

Generally, however, 1995 will be a positive and fulfilling year for the Tiger. By promoting his ideas and setting about his activities in a determined and persistent manner he can make considerable progress, especially in his work. And while financial matters and travel arrangements do need careful handling, his domestic and social life will give him much pleasure. The Year of the Pig is a year which holds considerable potential for the Tiger and it rests with him to act positively and to make the most of the favourable trends that prevail.

As far as the different types of Tiger are concerned, 1995 will be a generally pleasing year for the *Metal Tiger*. He will make substantial progress in his career and would do well to promote his ideas, skills and talents. By being bold and pursuing any opportunities that he sees, the Metal

Tiger will do well. Many Metal Tigers will be successful in gaining a better job or being promoted over the year. Financial matters do, however, need careful handling and even though the Metal Tiger may consider himself financially secure, he would still do well to watch his level of outgoings – they could be much greater than he thought! He will lead an enjoyable social life and strike up several new and valuable friendships over the year. His family life will, however, keep him fairly occupied and there will be several matters that will require his attention. These could include arranging a family function or helping to sort out some problems that a relation may have. Although at the time this could put the Metal Tiger under pressure, any support and advice he is able to offer will be greatly valued. Generally, however, much of the year will be a pleasant and constructive time for the Metal Tiger and he will make positive progress in many of his activities. With his inventive and creative flair it is an ideal time for him to advance his ideas, proceed with his plans and make the most of his many capabilities. For the bold and determined Metal Tiger, this can be a most successful and rewarding year.

This year holds a lot of potential for the *Water Tiger*. However, to take advantage of the favourable trends that prevail, he needs to decide on his priorities for the next 12 months. These may concern his work, his interests or his accommodation, but, whatever the area, he will find that by giving himself special targets to go after he will achieve more pleasing and worthwhile results than if he just drifts through the year without any particular objective. This is a year for positive action and, with a determined attitude, the Water Tiger can make great progress. He should advance any ideas that he has and follow up any opportunities for new jobs or promotion that he sees, especially in the first half of the year. Positive action will lead to positive results. The Water Tiger will also be helped by the generally co-operative and supportive attitude of those around him, and he should not hesitate to involve others in his plans. His domestic and social life will give him much pleasure and he is likely to find himself much in demand with his family and friends. He may, however, have to deal with an awkward domestic issue over the year. While this may cause him some concern at the time, he would do well to express his views openly and, in case of disagreement, come to an amicable solution as quickly as possible. Any domestic problems are likely to be short-lived, but the Water Tiger would do well to deal with them as they arise rather than let them linger in the background. He should also be careful when dealing with financial matters and not commit himself to any large transaction until he has checked all the facts and implications. When dealing with finance and important paperwork, the Water Tiger needs to be both cautious and prudent. Generally, however, this will be a satisfying year for him and by setting about his activities in an organized and efficient manner he will be able to achieve much over the year.

This will be a satisfying year for the *Wood Tiger*. He can look forward to having some enjoyable times with his family and friends and both his domestic and social life will give him much pleasure. For those who are unattached there will be plenty of opportunities to meet others and make new friends, although where matters of the heart are concerned, it would be in the Wood Tiger's interests to let any new romance build up gradually. This way he is more likely to put the relationship on a secure foundation. For the Wood Tiger who is engaged or newly married, the year will contain much happiness and many memorable moments. The Wood Tiger can also make considerable progress in his work and for those seeking employment, there will be several excellent opportunities to pursue, especially in the early months of the year and during the summer. Many Wood Tigers will change their duties and responsibilities over the year and while they may at first be daunted by what is asked of them, the experience they gain will serve them well and lead to better things in the future. This year holds a lot of potential for the Wood Tiger and it rests with him to make the most of the opportunities that are available. He should try to resist jumping from one activity to another – sometimes he can be rather restless – for he will find that a more persistent approach will lead to better and more satisfying results. He also needs to be careful and restrained when dealing with financial matters and keep a close watch over his level of expenditure. He should also avoid getting involved in any risky or dubious enterprises – without care, he could easily end up the loser! Generally, though, the Wood Tiger will greatly enjoy the Year of the Pig. He will lead a good social life and there will be some new and interesting opportunities to pursue in his work, some of which will lead to even better positions in the future.

This will be a favourable year for the *Fire Tiger*. He will be able to devote much time to his family, friends and interests, and all three are likely to bring him much joy and satisfaction. Both domestically and socially this will be a happy year for him and he can also look forward to attending several memorable social functions. Any Fire Tiger who may have had some adversity to deal with in recent times, or who may be wanting to widen his circle of friends or lead a more active social life, should make every effort to go out more, get in contact with others and perhaps join a local society or club. He will be glad he did so. All Fire Tigers will see a noticeable upturn in their social life over the year. It is also a favourable year for the Fire Tiger to consider taking up an additional interest or hobby. He will find that the challenge this offers will be most satisfying as well as giving him many hours of pleasure. He could find a creative activity that would extend his skills in some way particularly enjoyable. He can also look forward to some pleasant breaks in 1995 but would do well to check his travel plans are in order before he leaves. He also needs to be careful in financial matters and avoid getting involved in any major transaction until he has checked all the details and implications to his satisfaction. Generally, though, 1995 will be a good year for the Fire Tiger and by setting about his activities in a positive manner he will find the year both fulfilling and enjoyable.

This will be an important year for the *Earth Tiger* and one in which he is likely to give much thought to his present position and to his future. When considering this, he should avoid coming to any hasty decision but take his time and seek the views of those around him. The ideas he develops will prove most important and give him a clear direction and goals to aim at. In recent years some Earth Tigers may have felt that they have been drifting without achieving very much; 1995 will be the year when this can be rectified. Once again the Earth Tiger can take control of his life and decide on his future objectives and priorities. Some of his ideas and plans can even be put into practice later in the year and in this respect, 1995 will prove both constructive and significant. In all his activities, however, the Earth Tiger will need to pay careful attention to his financial dealings. This is not the right time to take financial risks. He will, however, make positive progress in his work and many Earth Tigers will find that a skill gained over recent years will prove most useful. Also, if the Earth Tiger has a hobby, interest or special talent that he can put to some profitable use, he should do so. By promoting himself in this way he can do extremely well, although in all that he does, it is *he* rather than others who needs to take the initiative. The Earth Tiger's family will be a considerable source of pleasure to him over the year and he will also delight in the success enjoyed by a younger relation. He will enjoy any short holidays or breaks that he takes and he should use any opportunity that he has to visit or contact friends or relations he has not seen for some time. As with all Tigers, though, to avoid mishaps and delay, the Earth Tiger does need to sort out his travel arrangements carefully before he undertakes any lengthy journey.

FAMOUS TIGERS

Sir David Attenborough, Queen Beatrix of the Netherlands, Ludwig van Beethoven, Tony Bennett, Chuck Berry, Richard Branson, Mel Brooks, Isambard Kingdom Brunel, Tommy Cannon, Agatha Christie, David Coleman, Phil Collins, Jason Connery, Alan Coren, Tom Cruise, Paul Daniels, Emily Dickinson, David Dimbleby, Isadora Duncan, Dwight Eisenhower, Queen Elizabeth II, Roberta Flack, Frederick Forsyth, Jodie Foster, Connie Francis, Charles de Gaulle, Crystal Gayle, Susan George, Mel Gibson, Whoopi Goldberg, Goya, Sir Alec Guinness, Bryan Gould, Elliott Gould, Lord Howe, William Hurt, Derek Jacobi, David Jacobs, Caron Keating, Matthew Kelly, Sarah Kennedy, Dorothy Lamour, Stan Laurel, Ian McCaskill, Ramsay Macdonald, Ali MacGraw, Karl Marx, Marilyn Monroe, Demi Moore, Eric Morecambe, Lord Owen, Jonathan Porritt, Marco Polo, John Prescott, the Princess Royal, Suzi Quatro, Diana Rigg, Lionel Ritchie, Kenny Rogers, Sir Jimmy Savile, Philip Schofield, John Smith (MP), Sir David Steel, Pamela Stephenson, Dame Joan Sutherland, Dylan Thomas, Liv Ullman, Julie Walters, Oscar Wilde, Terry Wogan, Stevie Wonder.

29 JANUARY 1903 〜 15 FEBRUARY 1904	*Water Rabbit*
14 FEBRUARY 1915 〜 2 FEBRUARY 1916	*Wood Rabbit*
2 FEBRUARY 1927 〜 22 JANUARY 1928	*Fire Rabbit*
19 FEBRUARY 1939 〜 7 FEBRUARY 1940	*Earth Rabbit*
6 FEBRUARY 1951 〜 26 JANUARY 1952	*Metal Rabbit*
25 JANUARY 1963 〜 12 FEBRUARY 1964	*Water Rabbit*
11 FEBRUARY 1975 〜 30 JANUARY 1976	*Wood Rabbit*
29 JANUARY 1987 〜 16 FEBRUARY 1988	*Fire Rabbit*

THE
RABBIT

THE PERSONALITY OF THE RABBIT

There is no man, no woman, so small but that they cannot make their life great by high endeavour.
— *Thomas Carlyle: a Rabbit*

The Rabbit is born under the signs of virtue and prudence. He is intelligent, well-mannered, and prefers a quiet and peaceful existence. He dislikes any sort of unpleasantness and will try to steer clear of arguments and disputes. He is very much a pacifist and tends to have a calming influence on those around him.

He has wide interests and usually has a good appreciation of the arts and the finer things in life. He also knows how to enjoy himself and will often gravitate to the best restaurants and night spots in town.

The Rabbit is a witty and intelligent speaker and loves being involved in a good discussion. His views and advice are often sought by others and he can be relied upon to be discreet and diplomatic. He will rarely raise his voice in anger and will even turn a blind eye to matters which displease him just to preserve the peace. The Rabbit likes to remain on good terms with everyone, but he can be rather sensitive and takes any form of criticism very badly. He will also be the first to get out of the way if he sees any form of trouble brewing.

The Rabbit is a quiet and efficient worker and has an extremely good memory. He is very astute in business and financial matters, but his degree of success often depends on the conditions that prevail. He hates being in a situation which is fraught with tension or where he has to make quick and sudden decisions. Wherever possible he will plan his various activities with the utmost care and a good deal of caution. He does not like to take risks and does not take kindly to changes. Basically, he seeks a secure, calm and stable environment, and when conditions are right he is more than happy to leave things as they are.

The Rabbit is conscientious in most of the things he does and, because of his methodical and ever-watchful nature, he can often do well in his chosen profession. He makes a good diplomat, lawyer, shopkeeper, administrator or priest and he excels in any job where he can use his superb skills as a communicator. He tends to be loyal to his employers and is respected for his integrity and honesty, but if the Rabbit ever finds himself in a position of great power he can become rather intransigent and authoritarian.

The Rabbit attaches great importance to his home and will often spend much time and money to maintain and furnish it and to fit it with all the latest comforts – the Rabbit is very much a creature of comfort! He is also something of a collector and there are many Rabbits who derive much pleasure from collecting antiques, stamps, coins, *objets d'art* or anything else which catches their eye or particularly interests them.

The female Rabbit has a friendly, caring and considerate nature, and will do all in her power to give her home a happy and loving atmosphere. She is also very sociable and enjoys holding parties and entertaining. She has a great ability to make the maximum use of her time and, although she involves herself in numerous activities, she always manages to find time to sit back and enjoy a good read or a chat. She has a great sense of humour, is very artistic and is often a talented gardener.

The Rabbit takes considerable care over his appearance and is usually smart and very well turned out. He also attaches great importance to his relations with others and matters of the heart are particularly important to him. He will rarely be short of admirers and will often have several serious romances before he settles down. The Rabbit is not the most faithful of signs, but he will find that he is especially well-suited to those born under the signs of the Goat, Snake, Pig and Ox. Due to his sociable and easy-going manner he can also get on well with the Tiger, Dragon, Horse, Monkey, Dog and another Rabbit, but the Rabbit will feel ill-at-ease with the Rat and Rooster as both these signs tend to speak their mind and be critical in their comments, and the Rabbit just loathes any form of criticism or unpleasantness.

The Rabbit is usually lucky in life and often has the happy knack of being in the right place at the right time. He is talented and quick-witted, but he does sometimes put pleasure before work, and wherever possible will tend to opt for the easy life. He can at times be a little reserved and suspicious of the motives of others, but generally the Rabbit will lead a long and contented life and one which – as far as possible – will be free of strife and discord.

THE FIVE DIFFERENT TYPES OF RABBIT

In addition to the 12 signs of the Chinese zodiac, there are five elements and these have a strengthening or moderating influence on the sign. The effects of the five elements on the Rabbit are described below, together with the years in which the elements were exercising their influence. Therefore all Rabbits born in 1951 are Metal Rabbits, those born in 1903 and 1963 are Water Rabbits, and so on.

Metal Rabbit: 1951

This Rabbit is capable, ambitious and has very definite views on what he wants to achieve in life. He can occasionally appear reserved and aloof, but this is mainly because he likes to keep his thoughts and ideas to himself. He has a very quick and alert mind and is particularly shrewd in business matters. He can also be very cunning in his actions. The Metal Rabbit has a good appreciation of the arts and likes to mix in the best circles. He usually has a small but very loyal group of friends.

Water Rabbit: 1903, 1963

The Water Rabbit is popular, intuitive and keenly aware of the feelings of those around him. He can, however, be rather sensitive and tends to take things too much to heart. He is very precise and thorough in everything he does and has an exceedingly good memory. He tends to be quiet and at times rather withdrawn, but he expresses his ideas well and is highly regarded by his family, friends and colleagues.

Wood Rabbit: 1915, 1975

The Wood Rabbit is likeable, easy going and very adaptable. He prefers to work in groups rather than on his own and likes to have the support and encouragement of others. He can, however, be rather reticent in expressing his views and it would be in his own interests to become a little more open and forthright and let others know how he feels on certain matters. He usually has many friends and enjoys an active social life. He is noted for his generosity.

Fire Rabbit: 1927, 1987

The Fire Rabbit has a friendly, outgoing personality. He likes socializing and being on good terms with everyone. He is discreet and diplomatic and has a very good understanding of human nature. He is also strong-willed and provided he has the necessary backing and support he can go far in life. He does not, however, suffer adversity well and can become moody and depressed when things are not working out as he would like. The Fire Rabbit is very intuitive and there are some who are even noted for their psychic ability. The Fire Rabbit has a particularly good manner with children.

Earth Rabbit: 1939

The Earth Rabbit is a quiet individual, but he is nevertheless very shrewd and astute. He is realistic in his aims and is prepared to work long and hard in order to achieve his objectives. He has good business sense and is invariably lucky in financial matters. He also has a most persuasive manner and usually experiences little difficulty in getting others to fall in with his plans. He is held in very high esteem by his friends and colleagues and his views and opinions are often sought and highly valued.

PROSPECTS FOR THE RABBIT
IN 1995

The Chinese New Year starts on 31 January 1995. Until then, the old year, the Year of the Dog, is still making its presence felt. The Year of the Dog (10 February 1994 to 30 January 1995) will have been a generally pleasant year for the Rabbit. He is likely to have made progress in many of his activities as well as having led a pleasant domestic and social life. For what remains of the Dog year, the Rabbit should continue to set about his activities in his usual conscientious way. Those around him will be most supportive and if he has any ideas or plans he wishes to advance he should do so. The last few months of the Dog year, from late October onward, will be a most positive and constructive time for him. He would also do well to deal with any outstanding matters, particularly correspondence, and to give some thought to his future objectives. Ideas that he develops now could prove important to him in the months ahead as well as giving him objectives and goals to aim for in the future.

Although the amount of time the Rabbit has for his own activities might be limited in the later stages of the year, if he does have the opportunity to investigate a new interest, or is able to make any enquiries about a subject he wishes to take up, he should do so. Anything constructive he can do – particularly anything that would extend his skills in any way – would be very much in his interests and could bring him considerable pleasure in the years ahead.

The Rabbit can also look forward to attending several most enjoyable social functions towards the end of the year. At some of these he will be able to extend his circle of acquaintances and some of those he meets could prove helpful to him in the future. Matters of the heart are also well aspected and the unattached Rabbit can look forward to leading an active social life, with new friends and romance. These favourable trends will continue through to 1995. Almost all Rabbits will find the last weeks of the Dog year a particularly enjoyable time.

The Year of the Pig starts on 31 January and is going to be a reasonably good year for the Rabbit. In some areas of his life the Rabbit will do particularly well, but in others he will need to exercise a certain amount of caution and restraint.

The most positive aspects of the year concern his relations with others. With his friendly and considerate manner, the Rabbit is highly regarded by others and over the year he will be much in demand with those around him. His family, in particular, is likely to give him considerable pleasure and not only will he delight in the achievements of those close to him but they will also give him much useful support and backing for his own ventures and ideas. He can also look forward to being involved in a family celebration over the year and for those who are unattached, the prospects for romance and for marriage continue to be highly favourable. Domestically and socially, 1995 will be a splendid year and the Rabbit can look forward to many happy and memorable times. Any Rabbit who may have felt lonely in recent times or may have had some difficulty to bear should make every effort to go out more and get in contact with others. If he does so, he will be pleased he made the effort and is likely to establish some new and important friendships. All Rabbits will see a noticeable upturn in their social lives over the year.

Many Rabbits will also consider carrying out some alterations to their home or garden in 1995 and while these will go well, the Rabbit should proceed slowly and carefully. If he is intending to do the work himself, he would do well to give himself sufficient time to carry out the project rather than rush things unnecessarily and end up with a less than satisfactory result. Alternatively, if he intends to ask others to carry out the work, he should make sure that he obtains written quotations beforehand and gives clear instructions about what he wants to be done. The Rabbit is likely to do much to improve and enhance his home this year, but these improvements do need to be thought out carefully and DIY projects in particular should not be hurried.

The Rabbit also needs to exercise care in work and financial matters over the year. Although he is usually most conscientious in his various undertakings, he should avoid taking unnecessary risks or acting without having first made sure he has the support of others. Progress in his work is possible – and indeed many Rabbits will do well over the year – but this will only come about by careful planning, preparation and concentrated effort. This is not a year for the Rabbit to trust his luck too far or to take unnecessary risks.

For those Rabbits seeking work or wanting to change their present position, there will be several good opportunities to pursue, especially in the first half of the year. Also, if the Rabbit is able to extend his skills in any way and add to his experience by home study or by enrolling on a course, he will find that this will do much to enhance his future prospects. Academic matters are also well aspected during the year.

As far as financial matters are concerned, the Rabbit will again need to proceed carefully and avoid taking unnecessary risks. If he intends to enter into a large transaction he should make sure he can meet all the obligations he may be placed under. Admittedly the Rabbit is one of the most financially astute of the Chinese signs, but in 1995 he does need to exercise care and leave nothing to chance.

The Rabbit will, however, derive much pleasure from his hobbies and interests over the year. The Pig year very much favours creative and artistic pursuits and for those Rabbits who are interested in these areas – and most Rabbits do have artistic skills – this is the time to take the initiative and to bring their talents to the attention of others. Many Rabbits will also find that one of their hobbies or skills could prove lucrative and may well open up new opportunities for them.

There will also be several opportunities for the Rabbit to travel over the year and he is likely to enjoy any holidays or breaks that he is able to take. Generally, this will be a favourable year for the Rabbit, particularly socially and domestically. His circle of friends will increase quite substantially and many Rabbits will have good cause for a personal or family celebration. The aspects are especially favourable for romance and marriage. However, despite these pleasing trends, the Rabbit does need to proceed cautiously in his business and financial dealings and avoid taking unnecessary risks. If he can bear this in mind, 1995 will be a most pleasing year for him.

As far as the different types of Rabbit are concerned, 1995 will be a reasonably good year for the *Metal Rabbit*. Although he may not achieve as much as he would like and may have some obstacles to overcome, he will still be able to make steady progress in most of his activities. He will find those around him supportive and it would be very much in his interests to seek the views and opinions of others before embarking on any new and major commitment. Throughout the year the Metal Rabbit needs to work closely with others and take notice of their views. If he can do this, he will find his progress considerably greater than if he were to try to set about his activities single-handed. Also, if he meets with any opposition to his plans or has a difference of opinion with someone, he would do well to adopt a conciliatory approach and try to reach a compromise. To let any disagreement linger on in the background would prove a distraction and waste his time and energy when he could be doing something more useful. Likewise, if some of his plans do not work out, he would do well to look at the reason why. By taking a constructive approach, he will be able to improve and strengthen his ideas and also avoid making the same mistake twice. In his work he will see several excellent opportunities to pursue and many Metal Rabbits will change their duties over the year. The Metal Rabbit would also do well to take advantage of any opportunity he has to widen his experience and increase his skills. Those Metal Rabbits seeking work should again follow up any openings they see. It may also prove worthwhile for them to look at types of work that they might not have considered before. The Metal Rabbit has many talents and can quite often succeed in areas where he might at first have thought he had no aptitude. He does, however, need to exercise caution when dealing with financial matters and should be wary of over-committing himself. Socially and domestically, this will be a most enjoyable and memorable year for him.

This will be an important year for the *Water Rabbit* and one in which he will see several changes. These could concern his work, his accommodation or his personal situation and, while some of the changes may cause him moments of anxiety, the Water Rabbit will emerge from the year in a stronger position and with some satisfying gains to his credit. He will find that out of change will come new opportunities and new challenges, both of which he will find stimulating and will give him an added incentive to make the most of his abilities. Indeed, if he has felt that he has been in a rut in recent years or has drifted without achieving very much, this will change in 1995. This will be the year when he can embark on something new and, providing he is prepared to be flexible in his outlook and maintain a determined spirit, his achievements can be quite considerable. If the Water Rabbit is seeking employment or would like to change his work, then he should actively pursue any opportunities that he sees. Similarly, if he wishes to move, he should start to look for new accommodation. However, while significant and positive changes will take place over the year, the Water Rabbit should not rush into any sudden decision just for the sake of it. Time is on his side and he will also find that those around him will give him valuable advice and reassurance if he does have any uncertainties. Throughout the year the Water Rabbit does, however, need to be careful in his financial undertakings and to make sure that he understands the implications of any large transaction that he enters. Socially and domestically, 1995 will be a splendid year for him and he can look forward to some pleasing times with his family and friends. The Water Rabbit will also enjoy any travelling that he undertakes and if he is creatively inclined, he would do well to promote and further his talents. For the bold and determined Water Rabbit, this can be a most exciting and stimulating year, full of new – and sometimes unexpected – opportunities!

This will be a good year for the *Wood Rabbit*. He can look forward to leading an active social life and romance is particularly well aspected. Many Wood Rabbits will get engaged or married in the year and, from a personal point of view, 1995 will contain many happy and memorable moments. It will also be a busy time for the Wood Rabbit and he will find it helpful to have some idea of his priorities for the year rather than squandering his energies on trying to do just too much. Should he feel he needs further assistance, he will find those around him most willing to help. In his work, the Wood Rabbit will do well and many Wood Rabbits will be successful in getting a better job and in changing their responsibilities over the year. Anything that the Wood Rabbit can do to widen his experience will be to his benefit and academic matters are also favourably aspected. Any Wood Rabbit who is involved in the creative arts or who has creative aspirations should also make every effort to promote his work as much as he can. This year favours cultural pursuits and with his many talents the Wood Rabbit could be a main beneficiary of these favourable trends. He does, however, need to deal with financial matters with care and with several expensive events likely over the year – especially if he gets married, increases his family or buys a house – it would be in his interests to keep a watchful eye over his level of expenditure. Generally, however, this will be a positive and constructive year for the Wood Rabbit and it will contain much happiness for him.

This can be a pleasant and relatively good year for the *Fire Rabbit*, although much of what happens in 1995 is heavily dependent upon him and his own attitude. During the year he should continue to set about his various activities in his usual determined spirit. He will obtain much satisfaction from his hobbies and interests and outdoor activities are also well aspected. If he enjoys travel, walking, gardening or following sport, then the year will hold many happy moments. Naturally no year is without its problems and the Fire Rabbit will have to contend with several of them – possibly of a bureaucratic nature – in

1995. In dealing with them, he should not hesitate to seek the opinions and advice of those around him. He has his family and many good friends to turn to for help and advice, and he will find much truth in the saying, 'A worry shared is a worry halved.' Fortunately, any problems that do occur are more likely to be nigglesome than serious and the Fire Rabbit should not let them get the better of him. He does, however, need to be careful when dealing with money matters and should avoid being pressurized into taking any action or entering into any financial under-taking against his better judgement. Time is on his side and if he has any reservations about a financial matter he would do well to wait or seek professional advice. His family and friends will be a great source of pleasure to him and he will be particularly proud of the achievements of a younger relation. He can also look forward to attending several most enjoyable social functions over the year.

This will be an interesting and generally satisfying year for the *Earth Rabbit*. He will lead a most pleasant social and domestic life and will be much in demand with his family and friends. He will also make a number of new acquaintances over the year and some of these will prove most helpful to him in the next few years, especially in relation to his work. The Earth Rabbit will also get much pleasure from his hobbies and he would do well to make sure that he sets a regular time aside for his own interests, particularly for any that give him a change from his usual daytime activities. He will also find that if he is able to take any short breaks over the year these will be most beneficial for him. The Earth Rabbit can make progress in his work, although he would do well to concentrate his efforts on areas that are familiar to him rather than try anything too diverse or ambitious. The summer months are likely to be a particularly busy time for him and those Earth Rabbits seeking work or looking for a change in their position will find that it is during the summer that their efforts are most successful. The Earth Rabbit does, however, need to exercise caution in financial matters and avoid getting involved in any speculative undertakings. Although he is usually astute in financial matters, this is not a year when he can take risks in money matters or trust his luck too far. Generally, however, he will be content with his progress over the year, but he is likely to get the most pleasure and satisfaction from his family and friends. Socially, this will be a most enjoyable year for him and for those Earth Rabbits who may have felt lonely or dispirited in recent years, 1995 will see a distinct improvement in fortune.

FAMOUS RABBITS

Prince Albert, Cecil Beaton, Harry Belafonte, Ingrid Bergman, Melvyn Bragg, Gordon Brown, Lewis Carroll, Fidel Castro, John Cleese, Confucius, Marie Curie, Kenny Dalglish, Peter Davison, Ken Dodd, Paul Eddington, Albert Einstein, Peter Falk, W. C. Fields, James Fox, David Frost, James Galway, Cary Grant, John Gummer, Oliver Hardy, Bob Hope, Whitney Houston, John Hurt, Clive James, David Jason, Anatoli Karpov, Gary Kasparov, Penelope Keith, Cheryl Ladd, Julian Lennon, Patrick Lichfield, Ali MacGraw, Trevor McDonald, George Michael, Roger Moore, Nanette Newman, Christina Onassis, George Orwell, John Peel, Eva Peron, Edith Piaf, Denis Quilley, John Ruskin, Ken Russell, Mort Sahl, Elisabeth Schwarzkopf, George C. Scott, Selina Scott, Sir Walter Scott, Neil Sedaka, Gillian Shephard, Georges Simenon, Neil Simon, Frank Sinatra, Dusty Springfield, Sting, Jimmy Tarbuck, Sir Denis Thatcher, J. R. R. Tolkien, Arturo Toscanini, Tina Turner, Luther Vandross, Queen Victoria, Terry Waite, Orson Welles.

16 FEBRUARY 1904 ～ 3 FEBRUARY 1905		*Wood Dragon*
3 FEBRUARY 1916 ～ 22 JANUARY 1917		*Fire Dragon*
23 JANUARY 1928 ～ 9 FEBRUARY 1929		*Earth Dragon*
8 FEBRUARY 1940 ～ 26 JANUARY 1941		*Metal Dragon*
27 JANUARY 1952 ～ 13 FEBRUARY 1953		*Water Dragon*
13 FEBRUARY 1964 ～ 1 FEBRUARY 1965		*Wood Dragon*
31 JANUARY 1976 ～ 17 FEBRUARY 1977		*Fire Dragon*
17 FEBRUARY 1988 ～ 5 FEBRUARY 1989		*Earth Dragon*

THE
DRAGON

THE PERSONALITY OF THE DRAGON

Either you reach a higher point today, or you exercise your strength in order to be able to climb higher tomorrow.
— *Friedrich Nietzsche: a Dragon*

The Dragon is born under the sign of luck. He is a proud and lively character and has a tremendous amount of self-confidence. He is also highly intelligent and very quick to take advantage of any opportunities that occur. He is ambitious and determined and will do well in practically anything which he attempts. He is also something of a perfectionist and will always try and maintain the high standards which he sets himself.

The Dragon does not suffer fools gladly and will be quick to criticize anyone or anything that displeases him. He can be blunt and forthright in his views and is certainly not renowned for being either tactful or diplomatic. He does, however, often take people at their word and can occasionally be rather gullible. If he ever feels that his trust has been abused or his dignity wounded he can sometimes become very bitter and it will take him a long time to forgive and forget.

The Dragon is usually very outgoing and is particularly adept at attracting attention and publicity. He enjoys being in the limelight and is often at his best when he is confronted by a difficult problem or tense situation. In some respects he is a showman and he rarely lacks an audience. His views and opinions are very highly valued and he invariably has something interesting – and sometimes controversial – to say.

He has considerable energy and is often prepared to work long and unsocial hours in order to achieve what he wants. He can, however, be rather impulsive and does not always consider the consequences of his actions. He also has a tendency to live for the moment and there is nothing that riles him more than to be kept waiting. The Dragon hates delay and can get extremely impatient and irritable over even the smallest of hold-ups.

The Dragon has an enormous faith in his abilities, but he does run the risk of becoming over-confident and unless he is careful he can sometimes make grave errors of judgement. While this may prove disastrous at the time, he does have the tenacity and ability to bounce back and pick up the pieces again.

The Dragon has such an assertive personality, so much will-power and such a desire to succeed that he will often reach the top of his chosen profession. He has considerable leadership qualities and will do well in positions where he can put his own ideas and policies into practice. He is usually successful in politics, show business, as the manager of his own department or business, and in any job which brings him into contact with the media.

The Dragon relies a tremendous amount on his own judgement and can be scornful of other people's advice. He likes to feel self-sufficient, and there are many Dragons who cherish their independence to such a degree that they prefer to remain single throughout their lives. However, the Dragon will often have numerous admirers and there are many who are attracted by his flamboyant personality and striking looks. If he does marry, he will usually marry young and will find himself particularly well-suited to those born under the signs of the Snake, Rat, Monkey and Rooster. He will also find the Rabbit, Pig, Horse and Goat make ideal companions and will readily join in with many of his escapades. Two Dragons will also get on well together, as they understand each other, but the Dragon may not find things so easy with the Ox and Dog, as both will be critical of his impulsive and somewhat extrovert manner. He will also find it difficult to form an alliance with the Tiger, for the Tiger, like the Dragon, tends to speak his mind, is very strong-willed and likes to take the lead.

The female Dragon knows what she wants in life and sets about everything she does in a very determined and positive manner. No job is too small for her and she is often prepared to work extremely hard until she has secured her objective. She is immensely practical and somewhat liberated. She hates being bound by routine and petty restrictions and likes to have sufficient freedom to be able to go off and do what she wants to do. She will keep her house tidy but is not one for spending hours on house-work – there are far too many other things that she feels are more important and that she prefers to do. Like her male counterpart, she has a tendency to speak her mind.

The Dragon usually has many interests and enjoys sport and other outdoor activities. He also likes to travel and often prefers to visit places that are off the beaten track rather than head for popular tourist attractions. He has a very adventurous streak in him and providing his financial circumstances permit – and the Dragon is usually sensible with his money – he will travel considerable distances during his lifetime.

The Dragon is a very flamboyant character and while he can be demanding of others and in his early years rather precocious, he will have many friends and will nearly always be the centre of attention. He has charisma and so much confidence in himself that he can often become a source of inspiration for others. In China he is the leader of the carnival and he is also blessed with an inordinate share of luck.

THE FIVE DIFFERENT TYPES OF DRAGON

In addition to the 12 signs of the Chinese zodiac, there are five elements and these have a strengthening or moderating influence on the sign. The effects of the five elements on the Dragon are described below, together with the years in which the elements were exercising their influence. Therefore all Dragons born in 1940 are Metal Dragons, those born in 1952 are Water Dragons, and so on.

Metal Dragon: 1940
This Dragon is very strong-willed and has a particularly forceful personality. He is energetic, ambitious and tries to be scrupulous in his dealings with others. He can also be blunt and to the point and usually has no hesitation in speaking his mind. If people disagree with him, or are not prepared to co-operate, he is more than happy to go his own way. The Metal Dragon usually has very high moral

values and is held in great esteem by his friends and colleagues.

Water Dragon: 1952

This Dragon is friendly, easy-going and intelligent. He is quick-witted and rarely lets an opportunity slip by. However, he is not as impatient as some of the other types of Dragon and is more prepared to wait for results rather than expect everything to happen that moment. He has an understanding nature and is prepared to share his ideas and co-operate with others. His main failing, though, is a tendency to jump from one thing to another rather than concentrate on the job in hand. He has a good sense of humour and is an effective speaker.

Wood Dragon: 1904, 1964

The Wood Dragon is practical, imaginative and inquisitive. He loves delving into all manner of subjects and can quite often come up with some highly original ideas. He is a thinker and a doer and has sufficient drive and commitment to put many of his ideas into practice. He is more diplomatic than some of the other types of Dragon and has a good sense of humour. He is very astute in business matters and can also be most generous.

Fire Dragon: 1916, 1976

This Dragon is ambitious, articulate and has a tremendous desire to succeed. He is a hard and conscientious worker and is often admired for his integrity and forthright nature. He is very strong-willed and has considerable leadership qualities. He can, however, rely a bit too much on his own judgement and fail to take into account the views and feelings of others. He can also be rather aloof and it would certainly be in his own interests to let others join in more with his various activities. The Fire Dragon usually gets much enjoyment from music, literature and the arts.

Earth Dragon: 1928, 1988

The Earth Dragon tends to be quieter and more reflective than some of the other types of Dragon. He has a wide variety of interests and is keenly aware of what is going on around him. He also has clear objectives and usually has no problems in obtaining support and backing for any of his ventures. He is very astute in financial matters and is often able to accumulate considerable wealth. He is a good organizer, although he can at times be rather bureaucratic and fussy. He mixes well with others and has a large circle of friends.

PROSPECTS FOR THE DRAGON IN 1995

The Chinese New Year starts on 31 January 1995. Until then, the old year, the Year of the Dog, is still making its presence felt.

The Year of the Dog (10 February 1994 to 30 January 1995) will have been a variable year for the Dragon. He is unlikely to have accomplished as much as he would have liked during the year and he could also have had several problems to overcome. For what remains of the year the Dragon will need to work closely with others, pay heed to all that is going on around him and keep a close watch on his impulsive nature. The Dog year is a time for caution, restraint and careful planning. The Dragon also needs to take care with his relations with those around him and remain tactful and diplomatic. The Dog year is not a year when he can afford to impair his relations with others – particularly when he could need their help in the future.

Although the Dragon could find the Dog year a frustrating time, he can take heart. His prospects will begin to improve from October 1994, and this improvement will gather pace and continue in 1995. He will also find that the experience he has gained in the Dog year – both good and bad – will serve him well. He will have learnt a lot about himself and his own abilities and this knowledge will help him deal with the opportunities and challenges that he faces in the future. For many Dragons the Dog year will have been an important period of learning and self-discovery.

In the remaining months of the year, the Dragon should

continue to deal with his activities in a restrained and cautious manner. He should be particularly careful when dealing with financial matters and should avoid taking unnecessary risks. He would also do well to give some thought to his present situation and to what he would like to accomplish over the next 12 months. The Year of the Pig will be a much better year for him and to take advantage of these improved trends the Dragon needs to know what to concentrate on.

Domestically and socially, the last few months of the Dog year will be a pleasant and busy time for the Dragon and any travelling that he undertakes will prove most enjoyable, especially if it leads to meeting friends or relations he has not seen for some time.

The Year of the Pig begins on 31 January and is going to be a greatly improved year for the Dragon. Some areas of his life will be particularly successful and his level of progress will help to compensate for any disappointments he may have had in recent times. The Dragon should, however, have a clear idea of what he would like to achieve over the year and work purposefully towards those goals. If he is seeking a job, a change in his work or additional responsibilities, he should actively pursue any opportunities that he sees. Throughout the year the Dragon needs to be bold and determined and even if he does meet with the occasional set-back or reversal he should strengthen his resolve rather than give up. The Dragon can achieve much in 1995 and it rests with him to be persistent in his various activities.

There will be several excellent opportunities for the Dragon to pursue in his work and one of these will occur very early in 1995. However, throughout the year the Dragon would do well to remain alert to all that is going on around him and follow up any openings that he thinks may be to his advantage. He will also be helped by the generally supportive and co-operative nature of those around him and he would do well to involve others in his plans and ideas.

In addition to the positive aspects in his work, financial matters will also be successful and the Dragon is likely to end the year in a much improved financial position. If he does have any surplus money, he would do well to consider investing some in a policy that would make provision for him in his longer-term future. He could find that this will turn into a useful asset in years to come.

The Dragon will lead an active social life over the year and attend some enjoyable functions. There will also be opportunities to make new friends and to extend his circle of acquaintances. Generally, his social life will prove most pleasurable. However, despite these positive trends, it is possible that the Dragon may experience a disagreement with a friend or relation over the year. If such a situation does arise, the Dragon would do well to sort the matter out as quickly and amicably as he can before it escalates. He does have a habit of being rather forthright in his views and in any fraught situation it may be in his interests to exercise a little more tact in some of the things he says!

For any Dragon who is unattached, there will be numerous opportunities to make new friends and the summer months are likely to be a particularly enjoyable time. However, the Dragon should be wary of building up high expectations in the early stages of any new romance.

Also, for some Dragons, affairs of the heart may not run as smoothly as they may like. However, while there may be moments of disappointment and anguish, most will find that after a set-back, new and brighter times will emerge, often quite unexpectedly!

The Dragon's family will offer him much useful support and encouragement over the year and he would do well to listen to any advice they are able to offer. They speak with his interests at heart and could well raise points that he may not have considered. The Dragon's family is always important to him and in 1995 this will be underlined by the help and encouragement they are able to give. The Dragon will also be able to take much delight in the success enjoyed by a close relation over the year.

One area where the Dragon does need to exercise care is with property. These words of warning particularly apply if he intends to move or carry out major alterations to his home. In either case the Dragon needs to proceed carefully, watch the costs involved and, if in doubt, seek professional advice. Without care and attention, matters to do with property could cause problems.

On a more positive note the Dragon will get much satisfaction from his hobbies and interests, particularly if they are outdoor activities or allow him to use his creative skills. He will also enjoy the travelling he undertakes, especially if it is to destinations which he has not visited before. Travel is well aspected in 1995 and many Dragons will cover considerable distances over the year.

Generally, this will be a favourable year for the Dragon and both work and financial matters are likely to go well. His domestic and social life will also give him much pleasure, although should difficulties in any relationship emerge, the Dragon would do well to deal with the problem as it arises rather than allow it to linger on. Property matters also need careful handling, but otherwise this will be an enjoyable and constructive year for him. It is a year for him to pursue his aims and to remain persistent and determined. For much of the year luck is on his side and for the bold and enterprising Dragon, great progress can be made.

As far as the different types of Dragon are concerned, 1995 will be a significant year for the *Metal Dragon*. If he has felt that he has been in a rut or not made much progress in recent years, 1995 will be a year in which he can make positive changes. Throughout the year the Metal Dragon should keep alert for new opportunities to pursue and not be reticent about advancing any ideas and plans that he has. This is a year for positive action and by setting about his activities with determination and his usual thoroughness, the Metal Dragon can make substantial progress. Many Metal Dragons will change the nature of their responsibilities over the year and any Metal Dragon seeking a new position would do well to consider areas that would widen his experience. He will find the challenge that this gives him will be stimulating as well as giving him an added incentive to make the best use of his many capabilities. February and March could prove important and significant months. The Metal Dragon will also be helped by the support and encouragement those around him are able to give. In particular, he could find a long-standing colleague or friend will be especially helpful and give him some advice or information which will prove of great value as the year progresses. The Metal Dragon will be fortunate in money matters over the year and he is likely to see an upturn in his financial position. He can also look forward to leading an active social life and any Metal Dragon who may have been feeling lonely or dispirited would do well to make every effort to go out more and get in contact with others. Any who are seeking changes and improvements in their current work situation also need to act. As all Metal Dragons will find, results in 1995 will come about by doing something positive. The Metal Dragon's domestic life will give him much pleasure this year and he will take great delight in the success enjoyed by a younger relation. However, despite the favourable trends that exist for him in 1995, there is still the possibility that he might find himself in a disagreement with someone over the year. As far as possible he would do well to try to sort the matter out as quickly and amicably as he can. Letting any disagreement continue unchecked will not only cause him much anxiety but could impair the normally excellent relations that he enjoys with those around him as well as taking the edge off what will otherwise be a good year for him.

This will be an interesting and varied year for the *Water Dragon*. He will make steady progress in his work and for those Water Dragons seeking employment or wanting to change their present position, the aspects are most encouraging. There will be several excellent opportunities for the Water Dragon to pursue over the year and he will find the skills and experience he has gained in recent years will stand him in good stead to make further advances. The spring and summer months are a particularly favourable time for career opportunities. The Water Dragon will also do well in financial matters and he might find it useful to conduct a review of his present financial position and make any alterations he feels necessary. He could be pleasantly surprised at the difference this could make to his financial well-being. The Water Dragon will enjoy the travelling that he undertakes over the year and any holidays that he takes will prove most beneficial for him. He will also be much in demand with his family and friends over the year and his social and domestic life will be busy and pleasurable. With his various commitments he may not have as much time for his own interests as he may like, but he should always try to make sure that he sets a regular time aside to relax and unwind and have a break from his usual daytime activities. He could find some additional exercise such as extra walking, cycling or swimming both beneficial and enjoyable for him.

This will be a positive and fulfilling year for the *Wood Dragon*. He can look forward to making considerable progress in many of his activities and he will also be able to advance his ideas and plans to his satisfaction. The Wood Dragon often has a very clear idea of his objectives and this farsightedness will help him considerably over the year. He should follow up any openings that he sees in his work and take advantage of any opportunity that he has to add to his skills and experience. If he is seeking work or wants to change his present job, he would do well to investigate types of work which he may not have fully considered before. By adding to his experience in this way he will do much to enhance his future prospects as well as opening up new opportunities which might not have been available before. This is a year when the Wood Dragon can explore his own potential and pursue his objectives and, with a positive attitude, his achievements now can go a long way towards helping his progress over the next few years. He will also be successful in financial matters and any Wood Dragons who have been experiencing financial problems in recent times will find their situation eased over the year. The Wood Dragon will lead a busy and pleasing social life in 1995 and his family will be a great source of pleasure to him. Many Wood Dragons will also have good cause for a family celebration over the year – this could be an addition to the family or success enjoyed by a close relation. The one area which could cause problems is if the Wood Dragon has a disagreement with someone, possibly a neighbour or work colleague. This dispute is unlikely to be serious, but if the Wood Dragon is not careful he could find it will prove an unwelcome distraction and take up much of his spare time. Fortunately, though, much of the year will be problem free and it will be a good, prosperous and enjoyable time for him. There will also be several opportunities for the Wood Dragon to travel in 1995, especially in the second half of the year.

This will be an interesting and rewarding year for the *Fire Dragon*. He will lead a busy and enjoyable social life and can look forward to attending many pleasurable functions. There will also be opportunities to make new friends over the year and while matters of the heart may not always run smoothly, the latter part of the year will be an especially happy time. Many Fire Dragons will also have good cause for a personal celebration over the year. Those involved in academic courses are likely to do well and anything that the Fire Dragon can do to further his skills and qualifications will be very much in his future interests. For those Fire Dragons seeking work or wanting to change their current job, there will be excellent and unexpected opportunities to pursue, particularly in the first half of the year. These opportunities will enable the Fire Dragon to add to his skills and provide some interesting, although perhaps initially daunting, challenges for him. In many respects 1995 is a year of discovery for the Fire Dragon and by setting about his activities in a positive manner and pursuing the opportunities he sees, he will not only do well but will learn a lot about himself and extend his experience and capabilities. One point that the Fire Dragon does need to watch, though, is adopting too intransigent an attitude. He needs to be prepared to adapt to new situations and be flexible in his attitude. If he can bear this in mind, his accomplishments over the year will be satisfying and worthwhile and will go a long way towards helping his future progress.

The *Earth Dragon* will enjoy 1995. He will be able to devote much of his spare time to his various interests and these will bring him considerable pleasure and satisfaction. He will also take delight in the successes and achievements enjoyed by some of the members of his family and domestically this will be a happy and contented year. There will also be opportunities for him to travel and he should take advantage of any chance he has to visit friends or relations he has not seen for some time. His journeys, travels and holidays will prove enjoyable as well as being most beneficial for him. The Earth Dragon will also do well in financial matters and many can look forward to receiving some additional and unexpected income over the year. An interest or special skill that the Earth Dragon has could also prove quite lucrative for him and if he can put it to profitable use, he should do so. If he intends to move or have any home improvements carried out this year, however, he does need to be certain of all the costs and implications involved. Without care he could find matters to do with property could cause problems and if he has any doubts he would do well to seek professional advice. However, despite these words of caution, this will be a generally satisfying, fulfilling and enjoyable year for him and could also contain some pleasant surprises!

FAMOUS DRAGONS

Jenny Agutter, Moira Anderson, Jeffrey Archer, Roseanne Arnold, Joan Baez, Peter Barkworth, Michael Barrymore, Count Basie, Stanley Baxter, Bill Beaumont, Saint Bernadette, Geoff Boycott, Tim Brooke-Taylor, Jennifer Capriati, Julie Christie, Kenneth Clarke, James Coburn, Bing Crosby, Roald Dahl, Salvador Dali, Robert De Niro, Susan Dey, Neil Diamond, Matt Dillon, Christian Dior, Placido Domingo, Fats Domino, Faye Dunaway, Prince Edward, Bruce Forsyth, Michael Gambon, James Garner, Sir John Gielgud, Graham Greene, Che Guevara, David Hasselhoff, Sir Edward Heath, James Herriot, Gloria Hunniford, Joan of Arc, Tom Jones, Martin Luther King, Ian Lang, John Lennon, Abraham Lincoln, Queen Margrethe II of Denmark, Yehudi Menuhin, François Mitterrand, Bob Monkhouse, Desmond Morris, Johnny Morris, Hosni Mubarak, Florence Nightingale, Al Pacino, Elaine Paige, Gregory Peck, Richard Pryor, Esther Rantzen, Christopher Reeve, Cliff Richard, George Bernard Shaw, Eduard Shevardnadze, Mel Smith, Ringo Starr, Princess Stephanie of Monaco, Karlheinz Stockhausen, Shirley Temple, Christopher Timothy, Raquel Welch, Mae West, Lord Wilson of Rievaulx (Harold Wilson), Frank Zappa.

4 FEBRUARY 1905 ～ 24 JANUARY 1906	*Wood Snake*
23 JANUARY 1917 ～ 10 FEBRUARY 1918	*Fire Snake*
10 FEBRUARY 1929 ～ 29 JANUARY 1930	*Earth Snake*
27 JANUARY 1941 ～ 14 FEBRUARY 1942	*Metal Snake*
14 FEBRUARY 1953 ～ 2 FEBRUARY 1954	*Water Snake*
2 FEBRUARY 1965 ～ 20 JANUARY 1966	*Wood Snake*
18 FEBRUARY 1977 ～ 6 FEBRUARY 1978	*Fire Snake*
6 FEBRUARY 1989 ～ 26 JANUARY 1990	*Earth Snake*

THE
SNAKE

THE PERSONALITY OF THE SNAKE

The right man is the one that seizes the moment.
                    – *Johann Wolfgang von Goethe: a Snake*

The Snake is born under the sign of wisdom. He is highly intelligent and his mind is forever active. He is always planning and always looking for ways in which he can use his considerable skills. He is a deep thinker and likes to meditate and reflect.

Many times during his life he will shed one of his famous Snake skins and take up new interests or start a completely different job. The Snake enjoys a challenge and he rarely makes mistakes. He is a skilful organizer, has considerable business acumen and is usually lucky in money matters. Most Snakes are financially secure in their later years provided they do not gamble – the Snake has the distinction of being the worst gambler in the whole of the Chinese zodiac!

The Snake generally has a calm and placid nature and prefers the quieter things in life. He does not like to be in a frenzied atmosphere and hates being hurried into making a quick decision. He also does not like interference in his affairs and tends to rely on his own judgement rather than listen to advice.

The Snake can at times appear solitary. He is quiet, reserved and sometimes has difficulty in communicating with others. He has little time for idle gossip and will certainly not suffer fools gladly. He does, however, have a good sense of humour, and this is particularly appreciated in times of crisis.

The Snake is certainly not afraid of hard work and is thorough in all that he does. He is very determined and can occasionally be ruthless in order to achieve his aims. His confidence, will-power and quick thinking usually ensure his success, but should he fail it will often take a long time for him to recover. He cannot bear failure and is a very bad loser.

The Snake can also be evasive and does not willingly let people into his confidence. This secrecy and distrust can sometimes work against him and it is a trait which all Snakes should try to overcome.

Another characteristic of the Snake is his tendency to rest after any sudden or prolonged bout of activity. He burns up so much nervous energy that without proper care he can – if he is not careful – be susceptible to high blood pressure and nervous disorders.

It has sometimes been said that the Snake is a late starter in life and this is mainly because it often takes him a while to find a job with which he is genuinely happy. However, the Snake will usually do well in any position which involves research and writing and where he is given sufficient freedom to develop his own ideas and plans. He makes a good teacher, politician, personnel manager and social adviser.

The Snake chooses his friends carefully and, while he keeps a tight control over his finances, he can be particularly generous to those he likes. He will think nothing of buying expensive gifts or treating his friends or loved ones to the best theatre seats in town. In return he demands loyalty. The Snake is very possessive and he can become jealous and hurt if he finds his trust has been abused.

The Snake is also renowned for his good looks and is never short of admirers. The female Snake in particular is most alluring. She has style, grace and excellent (and usually expensive) taste in clothes. A keen socializer, she is likely to have a wide range of friends and has a happy knack of impressing those who matter. She has numerous interests and her advice and opinions are often highly valued. She is generally a calm-natured person and while she involves herself in many activities, she likes to retain a certain amount of privacy in the things that she does.

The affairs of the heart are very important to the Snake and he will often have many romances before he finally settles down. He will find that he is particularly well suited to those born under the signs of the Ox, Dragon, Rabbit and Rooster. Provided the Snake is allowed sufficient freedom to pursue his own interests, he can also build up a very satisfactory relationship with the Rat, Horse, Goat, Monkey and Dog, but he should try to steer clear of another Snake as they could very easily become jealous of each other. The Snake will also have difficulty in getting on with the honest and down-to-earth Pig, and will find the Tiger far too much of a disruptive influence on his quiet and peace-loving ways.

The Snake certainly appreciates the finer things in life. He enjoys good food and often takes a keen interest in the arts. He also enjoys reading and is invariably drawn to subjects such as philosophy, political thought, religion or the occult. He is fascinated by the unknown and his enquiring mind is always looking for answers. Some of the world's most original thinkers have been Snakes, and – although he may not readily admit it – the Snake is often psychic and relies a lot on intuition.

The Snake is certainly not the most energetic member of the Chinese zodiac. He prefers to proceed at his own pace and to do the things he wants. He is very much his own master and throughout his life he will try his hand at many things. The Snake is something of a dabbler, but at some time – and usually when he least expects it – his hard work and his efforts will be recognized and he will invariably meet with the success and the financial security which he so much desires.

THE FIVE DIFFERENT TYPES
OF SNAKE

In addition to the 12 signs of the Chinese zodiac, there are five elements and these have a strengthening or moderating influence on the sign. The effects of the five elements on the Snake are described below, together with the years in which the elements were exercising their influence. Therefore all Snakes born in 1941 are Metal Snakes, those born in 1953 are Water Snakes, and so on.

Metal Snake: 1941
This Snake is quiet, confident and fiercely independent. He often prefers to work on his own and will only let a privileged few into his confidence. He is quick to spot opportunities and will set about achieving his objectives with an awesome determination. He is astute in financial matters and will often invest his money well. He also has a liking

for the finer things in life and has a good appreciation of the arts, literature, music and good food. He usually has a small group of extremely good friends and can be generous to his loved ones.

Water Snake: 1953

This Snake has a wide variety of interests. He enjoys studying all manner of subjects and is capable of undertaking quite detailed research and becoming a specialist in his chosen area. He is highly intelligent, has a good memory, and is particularly astute when dealing with business and financial matters. He tends to be quietly spoken and a little reserved, but he does have sufficient strength of character to make his views known and attain his ambitions. He is very loyal to his family and friends.

Wood Snake: 1905, 1965

The Wood Snake has a friendly temperament and a good understanding of human nature. He is able to communicate well with others and often has many friends and admirers. He is witty, intelligent and ambitious. He has numerous interests and prefers to live in a quiet, stable environment where he can work without too much interference. He enjoys the arts and usually derives much pleasure from collecting paintings and antiques. His advice is often very highly valued, particularly on social and domestic matters.

Fire Snake: 1917, 1977

The Fire Snake tends to be more forceful, outgoing and energetic than some of the other types of Snake. He is ambitious, confident and never slow in voicing his opinions – and he can be very abrasive to those he does not like. He does, however, have many leadership qualities and can win the respect and support of many with his firm and resolute manner. He usually has a good sense of humour, a wide circle of friends and a very active social life. The Fire Snake is also a keen traveller.

Earth Snake: 1929, 1989

The Earth Snake is charming, amusing and has a very amiable manner. He is conscientious and reliable in his work and approaches everything he does in a level-headed and sensible way. He can, however, tend to err on the cautious side and never likes to be hassled into making a decision. He is extremely adept in dealing with financial matters and is a shrewd investor. He has many friends and is very supportive towards the members of his family.

PROSPECTS FOR THE SNAKE IN 1995

The Chinese New Year starts on 31 January 1995. Until then, the old year, the Year of the Dog, is still making its presence felt.

The Year of the Dog (10 February 1994 to 30 January 1995) will have been a generally pleasing year for the

Snake and provided he has remained committed to his aims and objectives, he is likely to have made much progress over the year. Indeed, the Dog year is one of considerable potential for the Snake, although it rests with him to take advantage of the positive trends that exist. The closing months in particular can be a most satisfying time for him. There will be opportunities to pursue in his work and any projects that he has been working on or any ideas that he wishes to advance will be favourably received. The Dog year is a year for the Snake to act, be bold and remain determined.

There will also be opportunities for the Snake to travel in the latter part of the year and the journeys he undertakes will go well and could lead to some new and significant friendships. Both his family and social life will also give him much satisfaction and should the Snake have any uncertainties at this time he should not hesitate to seek the advice of those around him. The assistance he will be given will prove most useful and he should bear in mind all he is told.

There are, however, two areas that the Snake will need to watch. The first is that he must not be lax in guarding his personal possessions. There is a possibility he could lose or mislay something which he values and he does need to take extra care in looking after his belongings. The second area concerns his own welfare. For all his serenity and calmness, the Snake tends to burn up much nervous energy and the pressures and strains of the Dog year will have taken much out of him. It is essential that the Snake does not neglect his well-being and he would do well to make sure he eats a well-balanced diet, exercises well and also devotes time to activities that would help him to relax and unwind. If not, he could find himself feeling listless, tired and not enjoying life as much as he could.

The Year of the Pig starts on 31 January and is going to be a challenging one for the Snake. Throughout the year he will need to exercise a certain amount of caution in many of his activities and avoid taking risks. His progress may be slow and he may also have to contend with a few problems over the year. However, despite these variable trends, this will still be an important and valuable time for him.

During the year he will be able to give much thought to his present position and to what he would like to achieve in the future. The Pig year will be one when many Snakes will decide to shed one of their skins and look to new opportunities and fresh challenges. For many, 1995 will be a turning-point in their lives and, while the Snake's actual achievements over the year may be limited, the action he takes and ideas he develops will pave the way for his progress and success in the future.

In his work the Snake should continue to set about his duties in his usual conscientious way. He would do well to follow up any new opportunities that he sees and also use any chance that he gets to widen his experience and skills. If the Snake is seeking work or is unhappy in his present position, he should actively pursue any openings that he sees, particularly those that would widen his experience. He will feel stimulated by the change and challenge this gives him as well as do much to enhance his future prospects. Any Snake involved in the creative arts is likely to do especially well and he should promote his talents and work as much as he can. The year of the Pig does generally favour artistic and cultural pursuits and, with his keen and original mind, the Snake can benefit from this trend.

The Snake will also do well in financial matters and there will be opportunities for him to increase his income quite considerably over the year. However, he does need to be particularly careful when making investments and should avoid anything of a highly speculative nature. Although the Snake is usually adept in financial matters, 1995 is not a year for taking risks. Care is also needed if the Snake gets involved in any legal matter and if he does have any dealings with the law, he needs to make sure he obtains good professional advice.

For much of the year the Snake's domestic life will bring him pleasure and happiness and those around him will give him much useful support. However, he could still find himself having a difference of opinion with a relation or being involved in a clash of interests. In either case, the Snake would do well to sort the matter out as quickly and as amicably as he can. Even if he has to swallow his pride or give way on a certain point, this is better than allowing any awkward matter to sour relations.

A further problem could be caused by the Snake becoming so preoccupied with his work and own pursuits that he does not fully involve himself in the activities of those around him. In 1995 all Snakes, no matter how busy they are, should make sure that they devote sufficient time and attention to their loved ones. Although the Snake may value his solitude and a certain independence, he cannot allow this to get in the way of those around him.

The Snake can, however, look forward to leading a

pleasant social life and for those Snakes who are seeking new friends or are unattached, there will be plenty of opportunities to make new friends. Romance is particularly well aspected.

The Snake will also enjoy any holidays and short breaks that he takes and he will find outdoor pursuits particularly pleasurable. Although he may not travel too far in 1995, he will obtain much enjoyment from activities such as walking, exploring the countryside or gardening or from involving himself in sporting or other recreational activities.

While 1995 may not be the best of years for the Snake, provided he sets about his activities with care, avoids taking unnecessary risks and pays due attention to family interests, the year will be generally pleasant and constructive for him. However, he would do well to consider his present position and give some thought to his future. Although the Snake may not realize it at the time, 1995 will prove a significant year for him and his achievements over the year, together with the plans and ideas he develops, will herald the beginning of a new and fulfilling chapter in his life. For many Snakes, 1995 will be an essential stepping stone that will lead to the better times that lie ahead.

As far as the different types of Snake are concerned, 1995 will be a variable year for the *Metal Snake*. He could find that some of his activities are subject to delay and alteration and that it is difficult to make as much progress as he would like. However, while parts of 1995 could prove frustrating and disappointing, he will still gain much from the year and it will also hold some enjoyable times for him.

Throughout the year the Metal Snake needs to set about his activities with care and avoid taking risks. He also needs to be fairly flexible in his attitude and be prepared to adapt to changing conditions. By doing this, by setting about his activities in his usual conscientious manner and by remaining alert to all that is going on around him, the Metal Snake will gain much. He has a very perceptive nature and, while his progress may be limited in 1995, when conditions are more appropriate – which they will be towards the end of the year – he will be well placed to act and reap the rewards of his patience and his endeavours. In his work in particular, the latter part of the Pig year will be a most significant and rewarding time. The Metal Snake will, however, do reasonably well in financial matters and many Metal Snakes will see an improvement in their financial position as the year progresses. However, like all Snakes, the Metal Snake does need to exercise care in monetary matters and particularly avoid highly speculative or risky undertakings. His family and friends will give him much pleasure in 1995, although, in view of the busy nature of the year, he should try not to get so involved in his own concerns that he does not pay as much attention to those around him as he should. If he can encourage and promote joint family activities he will find this will bring much domestic happiness. The Metal Snake also needs to pay attention to his own well-being over the year and make sure that he sets a regular time aside to unwind and relax. He could find some additional exercise especially beneficial. While 1995 may not be the best of years for him, it will still contain some enjoyable times for him as well as opening up opportunities for the future.

This is going to be a demanding year for the *Water Snake* and he will have to work hard and concentrate on specific objectives in order to obtain the results he desires. The Water Snake has a determined nature and although he may face set-backs, delays and disappointments over the year, provided he is not deflected from his main aims, his efforts will hold him in good stead for the future. Indeed, many Water Snakes will not see the full results of their labours in 1995, but will find the work they undertake will pay off handsomely later on. In some ways, 1995 is a year in which the Water Snake prepares the grounds for future progress and some of the ideas and plans that he develops will prove most significant in the next few years. He will be generally fortunate in money matters in 1995 and, while he should avoid committing any spare money he has to speculative ventures, he would do well to consider investing in a policy which would make provision for his longer-term future. He will lead a pleasant social life over the year and any Water Snake who is seeking friends or is unattached is likely to establish a new and important friendship. He may, however, have to assist a relation who has an awkward problem to overcome. The support and attention he is able to give will be greatly valued. He should also make sure that he involves himself in the interests of those around him, as well as involving others in his own activities. Sometimes the Water Snake can be a little too guarded in his activities and this can prove irritating to others, especially when they are so keen to help him. Although he may not travel too widely over the year, any holidays and short breaks that he takes will be enjoyable and beneficial for him. While the Year of the Pig will be a challenging one for the Water Snake, his accomplishments over the year, together with the experience he gains, will serve him well for the future. This year is very much a springboard for his future success.

This will be a busy year for the *Wood Snake*. Although he may find progress in some of his activities difficult, he should not let himself be deflected from his longer-term goals and objectives. Many Snakes have found that before they realized their ambitions they had to overcome difficulties and that success only came after much effort and hard work – in 1995 the Wood Snake will be preparing himself for that success. Over the year he will gain much valuable experience as well as gaining a clearer insight into his future goals. He needs to continue to set about his work in his usual conscientious manner, seek out opportunities that are available to him and overcome – rather than be defeated by – any problems that occur. He should be wary of over-committing himself or trying to achieve too much too soon. Time is on his side and 1995 will be more a year for gaining experience and for planning rather than for action. The Wood Snake will be helped by the advice and support of his family and friends and if he does have any problems or uncertainties he should not hesitate to seek their advice. To try to deal with any worrying matter single-handed will only put increased strain on him – which, with the pressures of everyday life, he could do without. However, the Wood Snake will be much in demand with his family and friends over the year and both his domestic and social life will give him much pleasure. He will also derive much satisfaction from his various interests, especially any that allow him to use and further his creative skills in any way.

This will be a year of possibilities for the *Fire Snake*. Over the year he will give much thought to his present position and his future and in this he would do well to seek the advice and support of those around him. Even if he thinks he knows what he wants to do, he does not always have the necessary experience to achieve his aims and he would do well to listen to those who speak with experience. Also, some of his activities may not always proceed as he would like and this could cause him to review and amend his plans. Throughout the year the Fire Snake should be prepared to adapt to the events that occur – all the time he will be adding to his experience and learning about himself and his abilities and this will be to his future good. The Fire Snake should also be wary of trying to achieve too much too soon. He has many abilities, but to expect rapid results could lead to disappointments. Those Fire Snakes in academic work are likely to do well and will find that the time they devote to their studies will repay them handsomely. The Fire Snake can look forward to leading a busy social life in 1995 and for those who are unattached, there will be plenty of opportunities to make new friends and romance is very well aspected. The Fire Snake will also enjoy some good fortune in money matters over the year, although he does need to keep a watchful eye over his outgoings. He could find that some of the savings he has built up will quickly dwindle away if he is not careful. Although the Fire Snake may be faced with some uncertainties in 1995, the year will still contain many pleasurable moments for him. It will be one in which he will obtain much valuable experience as well as help to lay the foundations for his future success.

This will be a pleasant although demanding year for the *Earth Snake*. Some Earth Snakes will be tempted to move over the year and while those who do will be pleased with the eventual result of their move, the actual process could prove time-consuming and worrying. If the Earth Snake does move or wishes to carry out any other strenuous activity over the year, he should not hesitate to enlist the assistance of others. To take on too much physical activity or strain all at once could leave him feeling tired and below par. His family and friends are there to help if he asks. He will, however, lead a most pleasing social life over the year and any Earth Snake who may have been feeling lonely or dispirited should make every effort to go out more to meet others. He could find a local club or society just the tonic he needs, providing him with both a new interest and new friends. The Earth Snake will also take great delight in the successes enjoyed by a younger relation over the year and any encouragement he can give will be truly appreciated. He will also enjoy good fortune in financial matters, although he should avoid the impulse to rush into any major transaction unless he has checked all the implications involved. He should act in keeping with his usual meticulous nature and if in doubt seek reliable professional advice. The Earth Snake will enjoy outdoor activities over the year, particularly any day trips and short breaks he is able to take, especially if they are to places he has not visited before. He could find cultural pursuits particularly interesting and obtain much pleasure from visiting museums and other places of interest. If he uses his spare time wisely, this will be a satisfying and pleasurable year for him.

FAMOUS SNAKES

Muhammad Ali, Ann-Margret, Yasser Arafat, Paddy Ashdown, Edouard Balladur, Ronnie Barker, Kim Basinger, Tony Blair, William Blake, Heinrich Böll, Betty Boothroyd, Brahms, Jim Davidson, Bob Dylan, Stefan Edberg, Elgar, Mahatma Gandhi, Greta Garbo, J. Paul Getty, W. E. Gladstone, Graham Gooch, Princess Grace of Monaco, Linda Gray, Bob Hawke, Nigel Hawthorne, Denis Healey, Audrey Hepburn, Jack Higgins, Paul Hogan, Michael Howard, Howard Hughes, Rev. Jesse Jackson, Derek Jameson, Griff Rhys Jones, Gorden Kaye, J. F. Kennedy, Carole King, James Last, Cindi Lauper, Dame Vera Lynn, Linda McCartney, Craig McLachlan, Magnus Magnusson, Mao Tse-tung, Nigel Mansell, Dean Martin, Henri Matisse, Sir Patrick Mayhew, Robert Mitchum, Nasser, Bob Newhart, Mike Oldfield, Aristotle Onassis, Jacqueline Onassis, Ryan O'Neal, Pablo Picasso, Mary Pickford, Edgar Allan Poe, Michael Portillo, André Previn, Jean-Paul Sartre, Franz Schubert, Brooke Shields, Nigel Short, Paul Simon, Delia Smith, John Thaw, Dionne Warwick, Ruby Wax, Oprah Winfrey, Victoria Wood, Virginia Woolf, Susannah York.

25 JANUARY 1906 ~ 12 FEBRUARY 1907	*Fire Horse*
11 FEBRUARY 1918 ~ 31 JANUARY 1919	*Earth Horse*
30 JANUARY 1930 ~ 16 FEBRUARY 1931	*Metal Horse*
15 FEBRUARY 1942 ~ 4 FEBRUARY 1943	*Water Horse*
3 FEBRUARY 1954 ~ 23 JANUARY 1955	*Wood Horse*
21 JANUARY 1966 ~ 8 FEBRUARY 1967	*Fire Horse*
7 FEBRUARY 1978 ~ 27 JANUARY 1979	*Earth Horse*
27 JANUARY 1990 ~ 14 FEBRUARY 1991	*Metal Horse*

THE

HORSE

THE PERSONALITY OF THE HORSE

Let me tell you the secret that has led me to my goal. My strength lies solely in my tenacity.

– Louis Pasteur: a Horse

The Horse is born under the signs of elegance and ardour. He has a most engaging and charming manner and is usually very popular. He loves meeting people and likes attending parties and other large social gatherings.

He is a lively character and enjoys being the centre of attention. He has considerable leadership qualities and is much admired for his honest and straightforward manner. He is an eloquent and persuasive speaker and has a great love of discussion and debate. The Horse also has a particularly agile mind and can assimilate facts remarkably quickly.

He does, however, have a fiery temper and although his outbursts are usually short-lived, he can often say things which he will later regret. He is also not particularly good at keeping secrets.

The Horse has many interests and involves himself in a wide variety of activities. He can, however, get involved in so much that he can often waste his energies on projects which he never has time to complete. He also has a tendency to change his interests rather frequently and will often get caught up with the latest craze or 'in thing' until something better or more exciting turns up.

The Horse also likes to have a certain amount of freedom and independence in the things that he does. He hates being bound by petty rules and regulations and as far as possible he likes to feel that he is answerable to no one but himself. But despite this spirit of freedom, he still likes to have the support and encouragement of others in his various enterprises.

Due to his many talents and likeable nature, the Horse will often go far in life. He enjoys challenges and is a methodical and tireless worker. However, should things work against him and he fail in any of his enterprises, it will take a long time for him to recover and pick up the pieces again. Success to the Horse means everything. To fail is a disaster and a humiliation.

The Horse likes to have variety in his life and he will try his hand at many different things before he settles down to one particular job. Even then, he will probably remain alert to see if there are any new and better opportunities for him to take up. The Horse has a restless nature and can easily get bored. He does, however, excel in any position which allows him sufficient freedom to act on his own initiative or brings him into contact with a lot of people.

Although the Horse is not particularly bothered about accumulating great wealth, he handles his finances with care and will rarely experience any serious financial problems.

The Horse also enjoys travel and he loves visiting new and far-away places. At some stage during his life he will be tempted to live abroad for a short period of time and due to his adaptable nature he will find that he will fit in well wherever he goes.

The Horse pays a great deal of attention to his appearance and usually likes to wear smart, colourful and rather distinctive clothes. He is very attractive to the opposite sex and will often have many romances before he settles down. He is loyal and protective to his partner, but despite his family commitments he still likes to retain a certain measure of independence and have the freedom to carry on with his own interests and hobbies. He will find that he is especially well-suited to those born under the signs of the Tiger, Goat, Rooster and Dog. The Horse can also get on well with the Rabbit, Dragon, Snake, Pig and another Horse, but he will find the Ox too serious and intolerant for his liking. The Horse will also have difficulty in getting on with the Monkey and the Rat – the Monkey is very inquisitive and the Rat seeks security and both will resent the Horse's rather independent ways.

The female Horse is usually most attractive and has a friendly, outgoing personality. She is highly intelligent, has many interests and is alert to everything that is going on around her. She particularly enjoys outdoor pursuits and often likes to take part in sport and keep-fit activities. She also enjoys travel, literature and the arts, and is a very good conversationalist.

Although the Horse can be stubborn and rather self-centred, he does have a considerate nature and is often willing to help others. He has a good sense of humour and will usually make a favourable impression wherever he goes. Provided he can curb his slightly restless nature and keep a tight control over his temper, the Horse will go through life making friends, taking part in a multitude of different activities and generally achieving many of his objectives. His life will rarely be dull.

THE FIVE DIFFERENT TYPES OF HORSE

In addition to the 12 signs of the Chinese zodiac, there are five elements, and these have a strengthening or moderating influence on the sign. The effects of the five elements on the Horse are described below, together with the years in which the elements were exercising their influence. Therefore all Horses born in 1930 and 1990 are Metal Horses, those born in 1942 are Water Horses and so on.

Metal Horse: 1930, 1990

This Horse is bold, confident and forthright. He is ambitious and also a great innovator. He loves challenges and takes great delight in sorting out complicated problems. He likes to have a certain amount of independence in the things that he does and resents any outside interference. The Metal Horse has charm and a certain charisma, but he can also be very stubborn and rather impulsive. He usually has many friends and enjoys an active social life.

Water Horse: 1942

The Water Horse has a friendly nature, a good sense of humour, and is able to talk intelligently on a wide range of topics. He is astute in business matters and is quick to take advantage of any opportunities that arise. He does, however, have a tendency to get easily distracted and can change his interests – and indeed his mind – rather frequently, and this can often work to his detriment. He is nevertheless very talented and can often go far in life. He pays a great deal of attention to his appearance and is usually smart and well turned out. He loves to travel and also enjoys sport and other outdoor activities.

Wood Horse: 1894, 1954

The Wood Horse has a most agreeable and amiable nature. He communicates well with others and, like the Water Horse, is able to talk intelligently on many different subjects. He is a hard and conscientious worker and is held in high esteem by his friends and colleagues. His opinions and views are often sought and, given his imaginative nature, he can quite often come up with some very original and practical ideas. He is usually widely read and likes to lead a busy social life. He can also be most generous and often holds high moral viewpoints.

Fire Horse: 1906, 1966

The element of Fire combined with the temperament of the Horse creates one of the most powerful forces in the Chinese zodiac. The Fire Horse is destined to lead an exciting and eventful life and to make his mark in his chosen profession. He has a forceful personality and his intelligence and resolute manner bring him the support and admiration of many. He loves action and excitement and his life will rarely be quiet. He can, however, be rather blunt and forthright and does not take kindly to interference. He is a flamboyant character, has a good sense of humour and will lead a very active social life.

Earth Horse: 1918, 1978

This Horse is considerate and caring. He is more cautious than some of the other types of Horse, but he is wise, perceptive and extremely capable. Although he can be rather indecisive at times, he has considerable business acumen and is very astute in financial matters. He has a quiet, friendly nature and is well thought of by his family and friends.

PROSPECTS FOR THE HORSE IN 1995

The Chinese New Year starts on 31 January 1995. Until then, the old year, the Year of the Dog, is still making its presence felt. The Year of the Dog (10 February 1994 to 30 January 1995) will have been a generally positive year for the Horse and the closing months of the year are especially well aspected.

In what remains of the Dog year the Horse will lead a busy and enjoyable domestic and social life. He will be much in demand with his family and friends and can look forward to attending some splendid social functions. Any Horse who may have had some sadness or has felt lonely in recent times will find a distinct improvement in his situation and for those who are unattached, the prospects for making friends and finding romance are most favourable.

There will also be opportunities to travel and the Horse would do well to try and visit friends and relations he has not seen for some time. He will find these visits particularly enjoyable.

The Horse will continue to make progress in his work and the Dog year is a particularly good year for him to widen his skills and experience. If he is able to go on any courses or extend his skills in any way he will find that this will do much to enhance his prospects. The Dog year is very much a year of opportunity for the Horse and he should do all he can to further his interests and career. Positive action will lead to positive results. It is also a favourable time for academic pursuits and those Horses involved in education are likely to make pleasing progress.

The Horse does, however, need to remain alert to all that is going on around him in the closing stages of the year, as he could learn about an opportunity that will be to his future advantage. Also some correspondence he receives in December will bring some splendid news for him.

The Year of the Pig starts on 31 January and is going to be a variable year for the Horse. In some of his activities he can look forward to success, but in others he could face problems.

Looking at the more positive aspects first, the Horse can make considerable progress in his work. There will be several excellent opportunities which he can pursue and many Horses will take on new and more challenging responsibilities as the year progresses. The Horse will also be able to reap the rewards of his past endeavours; many Horses will be promoted or be successful in obtaining a better and more remunerative position. The early and later months of the year are particularly auspicious for career matters. As far as his work is concerned, the Horse needs to remain positive and committed to his aims and objectives. Those Horses seeking employment should pursue any opportunity they see and also take advantage of any training schemes or courses that they might be eligible for. By acting in this way, they will find their efforts well rewarded and many will be successful in obtaining a new position. This could be in a type of work which they have not tried before and which could lead to better opportunities for the future.

The Horse will enjoy an improvement in his financial position over the year and any Horses who may have been experiencing financial problems will find them easing as the year progresses. However, while financial matters are well aspected, the Horse should avoid being over-indulgent or squandering any spare money he might have. He could more usefully put it towards travel or home improvements or save it for the future.

The Horse's domestic life will be settled and content. However, he would do well to involve those around him in his various activities and also seek their advice over any matter that may be troubling him. Throughout the year his family will give him much useful support. The Horse can also look forward to leading an active and enjoyable social life and for those who are unattached, there will be many opportunities to make new friends. Romance and matters of the heart are likely to go well, especially in the summer months.

Many Horses will also devote some of their spare time over the year to their home, either in carrying out alterations or in moving. In either case, the Horse needs to exercise care. If he intends to move, it would be in his interests to keep a close watch on all the costs involved and also not be pressurized into making any decision against his better judgement. In any move, the Horse will eventually get what he wants, but it could take time. Those who intend to carry out home improvements should make sure they have a clear idea of what they wish to achieve and have the knowledge and equipment necessary to carry out the work. All activities concerning property and the home do need care and thoughtful planning, otherwise the Horse could face problems and disappointment as well as incurring additional expense.

The Horse also needs to take good care of himself over the year. Although he likes to keep himself active, he can sometimes overdo things and in view of the generally demanding nature of the year, he must ensure that he does not neglect himself. It would be very much in his interests if he were to put some time aside for a hobby or interest unrelated to his usual daytime activities, particularly one that would help him to rest and unwind. Also, if he relies a lot on convenience foods, he would do well to try to switch to a healthier and more balanced diet. Similarly, if he does not get much exercise during the day, he could find some additional activity such as walking, cycling or swimming will prove especially beneficial. Anything positive will do much to improve his well-being.

Naturally no year is without its problems and in 1995 the Horse will face several which could delay or cause him to alter some of his plans. While he will find this frustrating at the time, provided he is prepared to be flexible in his outlook and look constructively at any problems that arise, he will do much to defuse any awkward situation. Also, should he find himself in a disagreement with someone, he should try to adopt a more conciliatory approach rather than remain stubborn and intransigent. To prolong any disagreement unnecessarily could prove an unwelcome distraction and also affect the normally good relations he enjoys with those around him.

If the Horse can bear these cautionary words in mind, he will generally be content with his progress over the year. His work will bring him considerable satisfaction and his financial situation will improve as the year progresses. His social and domestic life will also prove pleasurable, but the Horse does need to deal with any awkward problems that arise with care and he should not neglect his own well-being. With a positive attitude, this can be a constructive, although not entirely trouble-free year for him.

As far as the different types of Horse are concerned, 1995 will be a generally satisfying year for the *Metal Horse*. However, like all Horses, he may face several problems over the year and have to re-think some of his plans. While at the time this may cause him some anxiety, he is sufficiently enterprising to turn difficulties into opportunities and make the best out of any awkward situation. By being flexible and continuing to set about his various activities in his usual conscientious manner, the Metal Horse can make progress over the year. His work and business-related activities are likely to go well and he could also be successful in finding another outlet for his talents. Money matters are also favourably aspected and many Metal Horses will receive an additional sum of money over the year for some work they have carried out in the past. The Metal Horse's family will be a considerable source of pleasure and pride to him and he will also lead an active and pleasant social life over the year. He will, however, need to be careful when dealing with property matters and be especially circumspect before committing himself to any major transaction. Similarly, if he intends to do any strenuous activity or handle potentially dangerous equipment, especially in DIY projects, he does need to take extra care. The Metal Horse will enjoy the travelling that he undertakes over the year and a holiday taken in the second half of 1995 will be one of the best he has had for a long time. He will also derive much satisfaction from his various hobbies and these will not only bring him into contact with others who share similar interests, but his knowledge could prove remunerative for him. While not all the events of the year may go entirely in his favour, the Year of the Pig will still hold many pleasing moments for him.

This will be a challenging year for the *Water Horse*. Despite his good intentions, he could find that some of his plans and aims do not work out in the manner he had hoped. This could apply to his work, his accommodation or some other activity, and while the Water Horse may feel frustrated by any set-backs that occur, he will find that out of disappointments will arise new and sometimes better opportunities. Indeed, by adapting to changing circumstances and retaining a positive attitude, the Water Horse can benefit from many of the events of the year. Problems and reversals will help to focus his attention on his present position and, given his resourceful nature, he will quite often come up with new ideas and spot new opportunities that he can turn to his advantage. This year will also hold several surprises for him and for some Water Horses this will involve a change in career or type of work. By being adaptable, listening to others and rising to the challenges the year brings, the Water Horse can accomplish much. He will be fortunate in financial matters and if he has any spare money he would do well to consider setting some aside for his longer-term future. He will lead an active and enjoyable domestic and social life over the year, although he would be advised to listen to any advice he receives from those close to him; there will be much wisdom in their words. The Water Horse also needs to handle official forms and items of a bureaucratic nature with care – a mistake or oversight could take a lot of time to sort out. He will enjoy any travelling that he undertakes over the year and, although he may not have as much time to devote to his interests as he would like, these will still bring him much pleasure and be an important source of relaxation for him.

This will be a pleasant year for the *Wood Horse* and while his progress may not be spectacular, he can still achieve much over the year. Throughout 1995 he needs to continue to set about his work and various activities in his usual conscientious manner. He should pursue any open-ings and opportunities that he sees and advance his ideas. While some of his attempts to improve upon his current situation may not work out as he had hoped, his efforts and talents are not going unrecognized and his persistence will eventually be rewarded, particularly in the second half of the year. The Wood Horse can also look forward to an improvement in his financial position in 1995. His social life will be most pleasant and many Wood Horses will make some new and important friends over the year. The Wood Horse's domestic life will be generally content although he may have to help a close relation deal with an awkward problem or may himself experience a difference of opinion with a relation or friend. In either case, a sensible, level-headed approach will do much to ease the problem. With the many demands on his time that he will face over the year, he should make sure that he takes at least one good holiday or break and gives himself a chance to rest and unwind and restore lost energy. He could find some of the journeys he takes particularly interesting, especially if they are places he has not visited before. Generally, 1995 will be a relatively pleasing year for the Wood Horse, with the second half of the year being a much more constructive and enjoyable time for him than the first half. He could enjoy some particularly good personal news in the closing stages of the year.

This will be a year of interesting possibilities for the *Fire Horse*. Over the year several events will happen which will cause him to look closely at his present position and to consider his future. In this he would do well to discuss his ideas with those around him and set himself targets or objectives to aim for. These could concern his work, personal life or some other activity, but the Fire Horse would be very much helped by having some plan to work to and sorting out his priorities. The ideas that he develops will help guide him to future progress and success. While not all the events that occur over the year may go in his favour, this will nevertheless be an important year for him and one which will herald the start of a new and positive phase of his life. His family and friends will be most supportive and he can also look forward to having some most enjoyable times with those around him. A younger relation in particular will be a great source of pride to him, although he may, during the year, have to assist an older relation who has some problem to overcome. The assistance that the Fire Horse is able to give will be very much appreciated. He will do well in financial matters over the year although, like all Horses, he does need to exercise care when dealing with property matters. If in doubt, he would do well to seek professional advice and also make sure he understands the implications of any agreement he is about to enter. The second half of the year will be more favourable than the first, with September marking a noticeable upturn in his fortunes.

This will be a generally pleasing year for the *Earth Horse*. His family life will give him many happy moments and he will be proud of the achievements and successes enjoyed by someone close to him. Socially, this will also be a good year. The Earth Horse will make several new friends and any who may have felt lonely in recent times should make every effort to go out more and perhaps join a local society or contact those who share their interests. By taking positive action, they will find their circle of friends and acquaintances will increase quite substantially and make this a much more fulfilling year for them. For those who are unattached, this could prove a most romantic year. Although the Earth Horse is unlikely to travel far in 1995, any holidays and short breaks that he takes will prove enjoyable and most beneficial for him. On a more cautionary note, however, he does need to take care when undertaking any hazardous or strenuous activity. If not, he could strain or injure himself and cause himself some unnecessary suffering. Throughout the year he would do well to remember the maxim, 'It is better to be safe than sorry.' Those Earth Horses involved in academic work will make pleasing progress and will find that the time they devote to their studies will be amply rewarded. If the Earth Horse does have any matter which is concerning him over the year, he should not hesitate to seek the advice of others. Those around him will prove most supportive and can do much to help the Earth Horse overcome or remedy any problem he might have. He would also do well to talk to those around him about his future – the ideas and plans he develops now will do much to help his prospects in the next few years.

FAMOUS HORSES

Neil Armstrong, Rowan Atkinson, Cheryl Baker, Margaret Beckett, Samuel Beckett, Leonard Bernstein, Sir John Betjeman, Karen Black, Helena Bonham-Carter, Leonid Brezhnev, Ray Charles, Chopin, Sean Connery, Billy Connolly, Catherine Cookson, Ronnie Corbett, Elvis Costello, Kevin Costner, James Dean, Anne Diamond, Clint Eastwood, Thomas Alva Edison, Britt Ekland, Linda Evans, Chris Evert, Harrison Ford, Aretha Franklin, Sir Bob Geldof, Billy Graham, Larry Grayson, Sally Gunnell, Gene Hackman, Susan Hampshire, Rolf Harris, Rita Hayworth, Jimmy Hendrix, Ted Hughes, David Hunt, Douglas Hurd, Janet Jackson, Nikita Khrushchev, Robert Kilroy-Silk, Neil Kinnock, Dr Helmut Kohl, Norman Lamont, Eddie Large, Lenin, Annie Lennox, Syd Little, Desmond Lynam, Paul McCartney, Harold Macmillan, Nelson Mandela, Princess Margaret, Spike Milligan, Ben Murphy, Sir Isaac Newton, Harold Pinter, J. B. Priestley, Claire Rayner, Rembrandt, Ruth Rendell, Franklin D. Roosevelt, Anwar Sadat, Peter Sissons, Lord Snowdon, Alexander Solzhenitsyn, Barbra Streisand, Patrick Swayze, John Travolta, Kathleen Turner, Vivaldi, Andy Williams, the Duke of Windsor, Tammy Wynette, Boris Yeltsin, Michael York.

13 FEBRUARY 1907 ∼ 1 FEBRUARY 1908		*Fire Goat*
1 FEBRUARY 1919 ∼ 19 FEBRUARY 1920		*Earth Goat*
17 FEBRUARY 1931 ∼ 5 FEBRUARY 1932		*Metal Goat*
5 FEBRUARY 1943 ∼ 24 JANUARY 1944		*Water Goat*
24 JANUARY 1955 ∼ 11 FEBRUARY 1956		*Wood Goat*
9 FEBRUARY 1967 ∼ 29 JANUARY 1968		*Fire Goat*
28 JANUARY 1979 ∼ 15 FEBRUARY 1980		*Earth Goat*
15 FEBRUARY 1991 ∼ 3 FEBRUARY 1992		*Metal Goat*

THE
GOAT

THE PERSONALITY OF THE GOAT

The world is a looking glass and gives back to every man
the reflection of his own face.
                    – *William Makepeace Thackeray: a Goat*

The Goat is born under the sign of art. He is imaginative,
creative and has a good appreciation of the finer things in
life. He has an easy-going nature and prefers to live in a
relaxed and pressure-free environment. He hates any sort
of discord or unpleasantness and does not like to be bound
by a strict routine or rigid timetable. The Goat is not one to
be hurried against his will but, despite his seemingly
relaxed approach to life, he is something of a perfectionist
and when he starts work on a project he is certain to give
of his best.

The Goat usually prefers to work in a team rather than
on his own. He likes to have the support and encouragement of others and if left to deal with matters on his own
he can get very worried and tends to view things rather
pessimistically. Wherever possible the Goat will leave
major decision-making to others while he concentrates on
his own pursuits. If, however, he feels particularly strongly
about a certain matter or has to defend his position in any
way, he will act with great fortitude and precision.

The Goat has a very persuasive nature and often uses his
considerable charm to get his own way. He can, however,
be rather hesitant about letting his true feelings be known
and if he were prepared to be more forthright he would do
much better as a result.

The Goat tends to have a quiet, somewhat reserved

nature but when he is in company he likes he can often become the centre of attention. He can be highly amusing, a marvellous host at parties and a superb entertainer. Whenever the spotlight falls on the Goat, his adrenalin starts to flow and he can be assured of giving a sparkling performance, particularly if he is allowed to use his creative skills in any way.

Of all the signs in the Chinese zodiac, the Goat is probably the most gifted artistically. Whether it is in the theatre, literature, music or art, he is certain to make a lasting impression. He is a born creator and is rarely happier than when occupied in some artistic pursuit. But even in this, the Goat does well to work with others rather than on his own. He needs inspiration and a guiding influence, but when he has found his true *métier*, he can often receive widespread acclaim and recognition.

In addition to his liking for the arts, the Goat is usually quite religious and often has a deep interest in nature, animals and the countryside. The Goat is also fairly athletic and there are many who have excelled in some form of sporting activity.

Although the Goat is not particularly materialistic or concerned about finance, he will find that he will usually be lucky in financial matters and will rarely be short of the necessary funds to tide himself over. He is, however, rather indulgent and tends to spend his money as soon as he receives it rather than make provision for the future.

The Goat usually leaves home when he is young but he will always maintain strong links with his parents and the other members of his family. He is also rather nostalgic and is well known for keeping mementoes of his childhood and souvenirs of places that he has visited. His home will not be particularly tidy but he knows where everything is and it will also be scrupulously clean.

Affairs of the heart are particularly important to the Goat and he will often have many romances before he finally settles down. Although the Goat is fairly adaptable, he prefers to live in a secure and stable environment and he will find that he is best suited to those born under the signs of the Tiger, Horse, Monkey, Pig and Rabbit. He can also establish a good relationship with the Dragon, Snake, Rooster and another Goat, but he may find the Ox and Dog a little too serious for his liking. Neither will he care particularly for the Rat's rather thrifty ways.

The lady Goat devotes all her time and energy to the needs of her family. She has excellent taste in home furnishings and often uses her considerable artistic skills to make clothes for herself and her children. She takes great care over her appearance and can be most attractive to the opposite sex. Although she is not the most well-organized of people, her engaging manner and delightful sense of humour creates a favourable impression wherever she goes. She is also a good cook and usually gets much pleasure from gardening and outdoor pursuits.

The Goat can win friends easily and people generally feel relaxed in his company. He has a kind and understanding nature and although he can occasionally be stubborn, he can, with the right support and encouragement, live a happy and very satisfying life. The more he can use his creative skills, the happier he will be.

THE FIVE DIFFERENT TYPES
OF GOAT

In addition to the 12 signs of the Chinese zodiac, there are five elements, and these have a strengthening or moderating influence on the sign. The effects of the five elements on the Goat are described below, together with the years in which the elements were exercising their influence. Therefore all Goats born in 1931 and 1991 are Metal Goats, those born in 1943 are Water Goats, and so on.

Metal Goat: 1931, 1991
This Goat is thorough and conscientious in all that he does and is capable of doing very well in his chosen profession. Despite his confident manner, he can be a great worrier and he would find it a help to discuss his worries with others rather than keep them to himself. He is loyal to his family and employers and will have a small group of extremely good friends. He has good artistic taste and is usually highly skilled in some aspect of the arts. He is often a collector of antiques and his home will be very tastefully furnished.

Water Goat: 1943
The Water Goat is very popular and makes friends with remarkable ease. He is good at spotting opportunities but does not always have the necessary confidence to follow them through. He likes to have security both in his home life and at work and does not take kindly to change. He is

articulate, has a good sense of humour and is usually very good with children.

Wood Goat: 1895, 1955

This Goat is generous, kind-hearted and always eager to please. He usually has a large circle of friends and involves himself in a wide variety of different activities. He has a very trusting nature but he can sometimes give in to the demands of others a little too easily and it would be in his own interests if he were to stand his ground a little more often. He is usually lucky in financial matters and, like the Water Goat, is very good with children.

Fire Goat: 1907, 1967

This Goat usually knows what he wants in life and he often uses his considerable charm and persuasive personality in order to achieve his aims. He can sometimes let his imagination run away with him and has a tendency to ignore matters which are not to his liking. He is rather extravagant in his spending and would do well to exercise a little more care when dealing with financial matters. He has a lively personality, has many friends, and loves attending parties and social occasions.

Earth Goat: 1919, 1979

This Goat has a very considerate and caring nature. He is particularly loyal to his family and friends and invariably creates a favourable impression wherever he goes. He is reliable and conscientious in his work but he finds it difficult to save and never likes to deprive himself of any little luxury which he might fancy. He has numerous interests and is often very well read. He usually gets much pleasure from following the activities of various members of his family.

PROSPECTS FOR THE GOAT IN 1995

The Chinese New Year starts on 31 January 1995. Until then, the old year, the Year of the Dog, is still making its presence felt. The Year of the Dog (10 February 1994 to 30 January 1995) is likely to have been a challenging year for the Goat. Over the year he may have found it difficult to make as much progress as he would have liked and may have had to contend with several problems. For the Goat, who tends to be a worrier, the Dog year could well have presented some anxious moments.

In what remains of the Year of the Dog, the Goat will need to remain careful and cautious, but he can take heart. There will be a gradual improvement in his situation and some of the problems that may have been worrying him will be resolved or considerably eased. His efforts over past months will now begin to be recognized and some progress, especially in work matters, will be possible. Also, while the Dog year may have been clouded with disappointments, the Goat will have been adding to his experience and this in itself will have made him a stronger and wiser person, something which cannot help but be to his future benefit.

The Goat's domestic and social life will, however, bring him much pleasure in the closing stages of the year. He can look forward to attending some enjoyable social functions and there will be opportunities to widen his circle of acquaintances. For any Goat who is unattached, the end of the Dog year could see the start of a romance which will truly blossom in 1995!

The Goat will also obtain much satisfaction from his various hobbies and interests and he would do well to make sure that he sets a regular time aside for recreational activities. Any Goat who has creative interests should actively further his skills and talents at this time.

While the Dog year could have been a generally disappointing year for the Goat, things will improve in the closing months of the year and this improvement will gather pace during 1995. November and December will be two busy but enjoyable months and if, at this time, the Goat is able to deal with any outstanding matters or correspondence, he will find that this will leave him freer and better placed to take advantage of the improved trends that await him.

The Year of the Pig starts on 31 January and is going to be a much better year for the Goat. His home and family life in particular will be a great source of pleasure. He can look forward to some enjoyable times with those close to him and there will be good reason for many Goats to hold a family celebration over the year. This could be through adding to the family, achieving a personal goal or receiving some exciting personal or family news. As far as possible the Goat should involve those around him in his various activities and seek their advice on any important decision he may have to take or on any matter that might be giving him concern. His family and friends will be most co-operative and over the year will give him much useful advice and support.

Socially, this will also be an enjoyable year. The Goat will lead a full and active social life and for those Goats who are unattached, seeking friends or romance, the prospects are excellent. Many unattached Goats will meet their future partner, get engaged or married in the Pig year, making this a splendid and memorable time. The summer months in particular will be especially happy.

The Goat's work prospects are also favourably aspected. He will be able to make steady progress in his career and should follow up any openings that might be available. Any Goat who feels that he is in a rut or stale in his present position should resolve to take positive action over the year and seek a more challenging position. Progress is possible, but it does rest with the Goat to take the initiative. The early months of the year will be a particularly productive time for him, although throughout the year the Goat will find that work matters will go well and that there will be some excellent opportunities for him to pursue. Those Goats seeking work should remain persistent and follow up any openings that they see. It may also be in their interests to consider types of work which they have not undertaken before – they could find the challenge this brings will give them an added incentive to do well and will also help them to widen their skills.

The Goat will also obtain much satisfaction from any creative activities that he carries out and some Goats could find that a skill they have will prove quite lucrative. For those Goats who are keen artists or writers, who are involved in the performing arts or who have a creative hobby, 1995 could prove a highly successful and rewarding year.

The Goat's financial position will improve over the year and any financial worries he may have been experiencing will be eased as the year progresses. However, despite the financial good fortune he will enjoy, he still needs to keep a watchful eye over his general level of spending. The Goat does have a tendency to be extravagant and without care he could find his outgoings are considerably more than he anticipated. Provided he is careful, however, he will end the year in a much healthier financial position than at the start. He is also likely to be fortunate in some purchases that he makes, particularly items for his home. By remaining alert he could obtain most advantageous prices. Any Goat who is a collector or who buys antiques should watch out for items of possible interest, for with his keen and perceptive eye, he could make some excellent acquisitions.

There will be several opportunities for the Goat to travel over the year, sometimes at short notice, and his travels will generally go well. A holiday or short break taken in the early summer will prove especially memorable and the Goat will also enjoy the many short trips and outings that he is likely to take.

There is, however, one area where he will need to exercise care over the year and that is with any important correspondence or forms he receives. He needs to deal with these promptly and carefully, otherwise he could find that there will be complications with bureaucratic matters which will take up much valuable time. All paperwork does need careful attention throughout the year.

Generally, however, the Year of the Pig will be a highly rewarding year for the Goat. His domestic and social life will be most enjoyable and many Goats will have good reason for a personal celebration over the year. This is a year of considerable potential for the Goat and it rests with him to take positive action and make the best of the favourable trends that prevail. For the bold and enterprising Goat this can be a most satisfying and successful year.

As far as the different types of Goat are concerned, 1995 will be a pleasant and rewarding year for the *Metal Goat*. He will lead an enjoyable domestic and social life and will be much in demand with those around him. Over the year he can look forward to several pieces of good news, either involving himself, his family or close friends, and generally the year will contain some happy and memorable times. He should set about his activities with renewed determination and many Metal Goats will be successful in realizing an ambition they have had for a long time. With a positive and determined attitude, the Metal Goat can accomplish much. He is likely to devote some of his spare time over the year to working on his home and garden and some alterations he makes will give him much satisfaction. He could also be successful in acquiring some items for his home which will be a great source of pride to him and, by remaining alert, he could spot some of these in the most unlikely of places. His many hobbies and interests will also give him much pleasure and outdoor activities in particular are well-aspected. He will enjoy the travelling that he undertakes over the year and could find shorter outings and visits to places of local interest especially enjoyable. In most respects this will be an active, happy and pleasing year for the Metal Goat and if he has had any misfortune or unhappiness in recent times, he would do well to consider 1995 as the start of a new and happier phase in his life.

This will be a profitable year for the *Water Goat*. In recent years he may have had some worries to contend with or faced several changes which have left him feeling uncertain about his future. In 1995 he will be able to put many of these uncertainties and worries behind him. This will be a year in which he can set about his work and various activities with renewed hope and determination as well as reaping the rewards of his past efforts. It is a time for positive action, when he can once again take control of the direction he would like his life to take. Whether it is a new job, promotion or a house move, whatever the Water Goat wants is possible – it simply rests with him to decide on it and then act. While he may not always relish change, those around him will be most supportive and throughout the year he should not hesitate to avail himself of this support. The Water Goat is likely to make positive progress in his work and he would do well to pursue any interesting opportunities that he sees, particularly in the first half of the year. He can also look forward to leading a content and settled domestic life and many Water Goats could have good reason for a family celebration. The Water Goat's social life will also be pleasant and he will attend several most enjoyable social functions during the year. He will also derive much satisfaction from his hobbies, especially if they involve him in outdoor or creative activities and provide a break from his usual everyday routine. The Water Goat will be fortunate in financial matters in 1995, although it would still be in his interests to keep a watch over his general level of spending. Without care, he could find this greater than he thought and extravagances could easily bite into his savings. Generally, however, 1995 will be a pleasing and productive year and if the Water Goat sets about his activities in a positive and determined way he can make great progress.

This will be a busy but satisfying year for the *Wood Goat*. He will make pleasing progress in his work and throughout the year he should remain alert for opportunities to pursue and ways in which he can put his talents to best use. For those Wood Goats seeking work or wanting to change their present position, the spring and late summer are particularly favourable times. The Wood Goat will also do well in financial matters and many will enjoy a considerable improvement in their financial situation. The Wood Goat's domestic life and home commitments will keep him busy but will also bring him much pleasure, especially through the achievements of a younger relation. However, there will be times over the year when he will feel under pressure and possibly even despair over all the demands that are being made on him. When this happens he would do well to decide upon his priorities and concentrate on these. By organizing his time well, he will be surprised at just how much he can accomplish over the year. Those around him will be most supportive and he should not hesitate to ask for assistance at busy times. Although he may not have as much time for his own interests and for socializing as he may like, he would also do well to make sure that he sets a regular time aside for recreational pursuits and to give himself the chance to rest and unwind. To drive himself too hard will only leave him tired and not enjoying life as much as he could. He could even find that if he were to take up a totally different interest this would give him a new and stimulating challenge and one which he would very much enjoy. If possible, the Wood Goat should also make sure that he goes away for at least one holiday over the year or several short breaks at different times of the year. He will find these most beneficial for him. Although 1995 will be a busy year, the Wood Goat will make considerable progress in many areas of his life and he should not hesitate to promote himself and his talents and pursue any opportunities he sees.

This will be an important year for the *Fire Goat* in terms of both his personal life and career. Domestically and socially, he will be very much in demand with his family and friends and he can look forward to some most enjoyable and memorable times. He could also see an addition to his family over the year or have some other good cause for a family celebration. He will also add to his circle of friends in 1995 and some of those he meets will prove most important to him as the year develops. The summer months will be a particularly active time for him and while there will be occasions when he will feel very tired, this is still likely to be an especially happy time for him. There will also be some excellent opportunities for him to pursue in his career and many Fire Goats will be successful in gaining a new position or of being promoted this year. However, in order to take advantage of these favourable trends, the Fire Goat must act positively and not be afraid of taking the initiative. If he is just prepared to bide his time or wait for opportunities to fall into his lap, he will miss some very good chances to improve upon his present position. This is very much a year that will favour the bold and determined Fire Goat, and for those who are prepared to make the effort, the rewards can be quite considerable. Throughout the year, the Fire Goat will find those around him most supportive and he should not hesitate to seek their opinion on his ideas or on any matter that may be causing him concern. Financially, this will be a generally good year for him, although he does need to keep a careful watch on his outgoings – he can sometimes be a little too extravagant or indulgent for his own good! Generally, however, 1995 will be a happy and fulfilling year for the Fire Goat and it rests with him to take advantage of the favourable trends that prevail.

This will be a pleasing and constructive year for the *Earth Goat*. If, in recent years, he has found it difficult to achieve his objectives or been disappointed with his progress, 1995 will be a year when he can put matters right! Throughout the year the Earth Goat should set about his various activities with renewed determination and vigour. The aspects are now much more favourable and he will be able to make progress in many areas of his life. Those around him will be particularly supportive and the Earth Goat would do well to enlist the help of others should he require it, or at least seek their views in times of uncertainty. Those Earth Goats involved in academic work are likely to do particularly well and the time they devote to their studies will be amply rewarded. These Earth Goats would also do well to give some thought to their future, especially to any skills or qualifications they might need for the type of work they want to follow. Their achievements over the year, together with the plans and ideas that they make, will help them considerably over the next few years. The Earth Goat's domestic and social life will also give him much pleasure and he can look forward to attending several very enjoyable parties and social functions during the year. The aspects are also favourable for romance and building new friendships, with the summer being an especially happy time. There will be several opportunities for the Earth Goat to travel during the year and the journeys he undertakes will go well and any holidays and breaks he is able to take will prove both enjoyable and beneficial for him. Generally, this will be a positive year for the Earth Goat and one in which he should make every effort to further and promote his skills and interests.

FAMOUS GOATS

Isaac Asimov, Jane Austen, Anne Bancroft, Boris Becker, Ian Botham, Elkie Brooks, Leslie Caron, John le Carré, Nat 'King' Cole, Catherine Deneuve, John Denver, Sir Arthur Conan Doyle, Umberto Eco, Douglas Fairbanks, Dame Margot Fonteyn, Anna Ford, Paul Gascoigne, Paul Michael Glaser, Sharon Gless, Mikhail Gorbachev, Larry Hagman, George Harrison, Sir Edmund Hillary, Hulk Hogan, Julio Iglesias, Mick Jagger, Paul Keating, Ben Kingsley, David Kossoff, Doris Lessing, Peter Lilley, Franz Liszt, John Major, Michelangelo, Cliff Michelmore, Joni Mitchell, Edwin Moses, Frank Muir, Rupert Murdoch, Mussolini, Leonard Nimoy, Oliver North, Des O'Connor, Lord Olivier, Michael Palin, Alain Prost, Keith Richards, Sir Malcolm Sargent, Mike Smith, Freddie Starr, Lord Tebbit, Leslie Thomas, Mark Twain, Rudolph Valentino, Vangelis, Terry Venables, Lech Walesa, Barbara Walters, Andy Warhol, John Wayne, Tuesday Weld, Fay Weldon, Bruce Willis, Debra Winger.

2 FEBRUARY 1908 ⁓ 21 JANUARY 1909   *Earth Monkey*

20 FEBRUARY 1920 ⁓ 7 FEBRUARY 1921   *Metal Monkey*

6 FEBRUARY 1932 ⁓ 25 JANUARY 1933   *Water Monkey*

25 JANUARY 1944 ⁓ 12 FEBRUARY 1945   *Wood Monkey*

12 FEBRUARY 1956 ⁓ 30 JANUARY 1957   *Fire Monkey*

30 JANUARY 1968 ⁓ 16 FEBRUARY 1969   *Earth Monkey*

16 FEBRUARY 1980 ⁓ 4 FEBRUARY 1981   *Metal Monkey*

4 FEBRUARY 1992 ⁓ 22 JANUARY 1993   *Water Monkey*

T H E
MONKEY

THE PERSONALITY OF THE MONKEY

> Whatever I have tried to do in this life, I have tried with
> all my heart to do well; whatever I have devoted myself
> to, I have devoted myself to completely; in great aims and
> in small, I have always been thoroughly earnest.
> – *Charles Dickens: a Monkey*

The Monkey is born under the sign of fantasy. He is imaginative, inquisitive and loves to keep an eye on everything that is going on around him. He is never backward in offering advice or trying to sort out the problems of others. He likes to be helpful and his advice is invariably sensible and reliable.

The Monkey is intelligent, well-read and always eager to learn. He has an extremely good memory and there are many Monkeys who have made particularly good linguists. The Monkey is also a convincing talker and enjoys taking part in discussions and debates. His friendly, self-assured manner can be very persuasive and he usually has little trouble in winning people round to his way of thinking – it is for this reason that the Monkey often excels in politics and public speaking. He is also particularly adept in PR work, teaching and any job which involves selling.

The Monkey can, however, be crafty, cunning and occasionally dishonest, and he will seize on any opportunity to make a quick gain or outsmart his opponents. He has so much charm and guile that people often don't realize what he is up to until it is too late. But despite his resourceful nature, the Monkey does run the risk of outsmarting even himself. He has so much confidence in his abilities that he rarely listens to advice or is prepared to accept help from anyone. The Monkey likes to help others but prefers to rely on his own judgement when dealing with his own affairs.

Another characteristic of the Monkey is that he is extremely good at solving problems and has a happy knack of extricating himself (and others) from the most hopeless of positions. He is the master of self-preservation.

With so many diverse talents the Monkey is able to make considerable sums of money, but he does like to enjoy life and will think nothing of spending his money on some exotic holiday or luxury which he has had his eye on. He can, however, become very envious if someone else has got what he wants.

The Monkey is an original thinker and, despite his love of company, he cherishes his independence. He has to have the freedom to act as he wants and any Monkey who feels hemmed in or bound by too many restrictions can soon become unhappy. Likewise, if anything becomes too boring or monotonous, he soon loses interest and turns his attention to something else. The Monkey lacks persistence and this can often hamper his progress. He is also easily distracted, a tendency which all Monkeys should try to overcome. The Monkey should concentrate on one thing at a time and by doing so will almost certainly achieve more in the long run.

The Monkey is a good organizer and, even though he may behave slightly erratically at times, he will invariably have some plan at the back of his mind. On the odd occasion when his plans do not quite work out, he is usually quite happy to shrug his shoulders and put it down to experience. He will rarely make the same mistake twice and throughout his life he will try his hand at many things.

The Monkey likes to impress and is rarely without followers or admirers. There are many who are attracted to him by his good looks, his sense of humour or simply because he instils so much confidence.

Monkeys usually marry young and for it to be a success their partner must allow them time to pursue their many interests and the opportunity to indulge in their love of travel. The Monkey has to have variety in his life and is especially well-suited to those born under the sociable and outgoing signs of the Rat, Dragon, Pig and Goat. The Ox, Rabbit, Snake and Dog will also be enchanted by the Monkey's resourceful and outgoing nature, but the Monkey is likely to exasperate the Rooster and Horse, and the Tiger will have little patience for the Monkey's tricks. A relationship between two Monkeys will also work well – they will understand each other and be able to assist each other in their various enterprises.

The lady Monkey is intelligent, extremely observant and a shrewd judge of character. Her opinions and views are often highly valued, and having such a persuasive nature, she invariably gets her own way. The lady Monkey has many interests and involves herself in a wide variety of activities. She pays great attention to her appearance, is an elegant dresser and likes to take particular care over her hair. She can also be a most caring and doting parent and will have many good and loyal friends.

Provided the Monkey can curb his desire to take part in

all that is going on around him and concentrate on one thing at a time, he can usually achieve what he wants in life. Should he suffer any disappointments, he is bound to bounce back. The Monkey is a survivor and his life is usually both colourful and very eventful.

THE FIVE DIFFERENT TYPES OF MONKEY

In addition to the 12 signs of the Chinese zodiac, there are five elements and these have a strengthening or moderating influence on the sign. The effects of the five elements on the Monkey are described below, together with the years in which the elements were exercising their influence. Therefore all Monkeys born in 1920 and 1980 are Metal Monkeys, those born in 1932 and 1992 are Water Monkeys, and so on.

Metal Monkey: 1920, 1980
The Metal Monkey is very strong-willed. He sets about everything he does with a dogged determination and often prefers to work independently rather than with others. He is ambitious, wise and confident, and is certainly not afraid of hard work. He is very astute in financial matters and usually chooses his investments well. Despite his somewhat independent nature, the Metal Monkey enjoys attending parties and social occasions and is particularly warm and caring towards his loved ones.

Water Monkey: 1932, 1992

The Water Monkey is versatile, determined and perceptive. He also has more discipline than some of the other Monkeys and is prepared to work towards a certain goal rather than be distracted by something else. He is not always open about his true intentions and when questioned can be particularly evasive. He can be sensitive to criticism but also very persuasive and usually has little trouble in getting others to fall in with his plans. He has a very good understanding of human nature and relates well to others.

Wood Monkey: 1944

This Monkey is efficient, methodical and extremely conscientious. He is also highly imaginative and is always trying to capitalize on new ideas or learning new skills. Occasionally his enthusiasm can get the better of him and he can get very agitated when things do not quite work out as he had hoped. He does, however, have a very adventurous streak in him and is not afraid of taking risks. He also loves travel. He is usually held in great esteem by his friends and colleagues.

Fire Monkey: 1896, 1956

The Fire Monkey is intelligent, full of vitality and has no trouble in commanding the respect of others. He is imaginative and has wide interests, although sometimes these can distract him from more useful and profitable work. He is very competitive and always likes to be involved in everything that is going on. He can be stubborn if he does not get his own way and he sometimes tries to indoctrinate those who are less strong-willed than himself. The Fire Monkey is a lively character, popular with the opposite sex and extremely loyal to his partner.

Earth Monkey: 1908, 1968

The Earth Monkey tends to be studious and well-read, and can become quite distinguished in his chosen line of work. He is less outgoing than some of the other types of Monkey and prefers quieter and more solid pursuits. He has high principles, a very caring nature, and can be most generous to those less fortunate than himself. He is usually successful in handling financial matters and can become very wealthy in old age. He has a calming influence on those around him and is respected and well liked by those he meets. He is, however, especially careful about whom he lets into his confidence.

PROSPECTS FOR THE MONKEY IN 1995

The Chinese New Year starts on 31 January 1995. Until then, the old year, the Year of the Dog, is still making its presence felt.

The Year of the Dog (10 February 1994 to 30 January 1995) will not have been the best of years for the Monkey and even in its closing stages he will still need to exercise care in his various undertakings. Over the year he could have found it difficult to make as much progress as he would have liked and may have met with opposition to some of his plans. He could also have experienced financial uncertainties and this too could have caused him additional worry.

In what remains of the Dog year the Monkey should avoid taking risks or getting involved in too many undertakings all at the same time. He will find that if he is able to plan his activities and concentrate on specific matters he will make far better progress. This particularly applies to any projects he is carrying out in his home or at work. But with a concerted and determined effort, the Monkey can achieve much in the closing months of the year as well as clearing up outstanding matters.

The Monkey will lead a pleasing domestic and social life at this time and will be much in demand with those around him. He can look forward to attending some enjoyable social occasions towards the end of the year and, for those who are unattached, a new friendship will bring much happiness. The Monkey will also obtain considerable satisfaction from his hobbies, especially those that enable him to get away from normal everyday pressures. Also, if he is able to take a short break in the closing stages of the year, he will find that this will be most beneficial for him and will leave him feeling fresher and more revitalized.

The Year of the Dog will have been a challenging year for most Monkeys, but the Monkey will still find that, despite the difficulties he has faced, his accomplishments and the experience he has gained will serve him well. He will have learnt a lot about himself, his attitudes and values, and he will be able to put this new-found knowledge to effective use in the future.

The Year of the Pig starts on 31 January and over the course of the year the Monkey will see a gradual improvement in his fortunes. Admittedly not all his plans may go as well as he would like, but he will enjoy both happy times and some good successes over the year.

The main points that the Monkey will need to remember in 1995 are not to expect instant results or to commit himself to too many undertakings at any one time. Success and progress will come through concentrating on specific matters rather than trying to be over-ambitious or to obtain results without the proper preparation.

The aspects are, however, generally favourable for the Monkey in his work. There will be some very good opportunities for him to pursue and many Monkeys will be successful in obtaining promotion or a new position. The Monkey would, however, do well to pay close attention to the views of his colleagues and not to adopt too independent an attitude. Although he is resourceful and likes to retain a certain independence in his actions, this is not a year when he can accomplish what he desires without the support of others. The early months of the year and October and November could see some good news concerning his career and he should use any opportunity in these months to advance his ideas or pursue any openings or vacancies that interest him. It would also be helpful if he were to give some thought to his longer-term career aspirations and if he finds that he is in need of some additional skills or qualifications, this would be an ideal year to start to obtain them. Anything practical and constructive that the Monkey can do will be to his future advantage.

The Monkey will also enjoy an improvement in his

financial situation and any savings he can put aside could turn into a worthwhile asset in years to come. Provided he is careful in his financial undertakings he can do well, but again this is not a year when the Monkey can afford to push his luck too far and take unnecessary risks with his money.

The Monkey's family life will be busy and content. He will take great pride in the achievements of someone close to him and he can also look forward to some pleasing family occasions. He would, however, do well to involve those close to him in his various activities and also discuss his plans and any worries he may have. Sometimes the Monkey can be rather evasive and has a tendency to keep his thoughts and ideas to himself. Such an attitude could prove detrimental in 1995. To make progress during the year he does need the support of those around him and this includes involving others in his activities. He would also do well to listen carefully to any advice he receives from those close to him; there will be much wisdom in their words.

The Monkey's social life will give him much pleasure and with his genial nature he will impress many over the year. The unattached Monkey in particular can look forward to an active social life and while there will be plenty of opportunities for romance and friendship, all Monkeys need to pay careful attention to the views and interests of their friends, otherwise they could find strains appearing in some of their friendships. Although the Monkey has a most persuasive nature, he cannot expect to have everything his own way and there will be times over the year when he may have to make concessions or compromise on certain matters in order to preserve good relations with those around him – and this applies to both family and friends!

The Monkey will, however, obtain much satisfaction from his various hobbies and interests and he would do well to set a regular time aside for anything that would give him a break from his usual daytime activities. Also, if he does not get much exercise during the day, he should consider doing some extra walking or some other suitable physical exercise such as swimming or cycling. He will find that any extra activity will do much to improve his sense of well-being.

There are, however, two areas which the Monkey will need to be careful with in 1995. The first concerns legal matters. If the Monkey should find himself in any difficulties over the year, especially anything that involves the law and legal system, he would do well to seek professional advice. Fortunately these words of warning will only apply to a very few Monkeys, but legal matters could cause problems and it is a warning that Monkeys would do well to remember.

The second area is of a more bureaucratic nature. Throughout the year the Monkey needs to exercise care with all important documents that he receives or has to complete. He should particularly be careful to check the small print of any agreement he has to sign and be aware of the implications of any agreement he enters into. Without care, paperwork and bureaucratic matters could cause problems in 1995.

Generally however, if the Monkey sets about his activities in an organized manner, is prepared to involve others and does not take undue risks, 1995 can be a positive and fulfilling year for him. He can make progress in many of his undertakings and his career and financial matters in particular are likely to go very well.

As far as the different types of Monkey are concerned, 1995 will be an interesting year for the *Metal Monkey*. He can look forward to a content social and domestic life and his family and friends will be a great source of pleasure to him. His social life is likely to be more active than it has been in recent years and he will extend his circle of acquaintances quite considerably. The Metal Monkey will also do well in financial matters, although he should still avoid any highly speculative ventures. Occasionally he can push his luck too far and 1995 is not a year when he can take unnecessary financial risks. He will, however, derive considerable pleasure from his various interests over the year, especially any which will allow him to expand upon his many talents or take him out of doors. Those Metal Monkeys involved in academic work will make pleasing progress and the time they devote to their studies will repay them handsomely in this and future years. These Monkeys should, however, give some thought to their future over the year and discuss their thoughts with those around them. Some ideas they develop now will prove very important in the next few years. Also if there is something that the Metal Monkey wishes to achieve, no matter whether it concerns a personal ambition, a visit somewhere or his future career, now is the time to plan and make enquiries. As he will find, he can make much progress over the year, but it will require positive effort on his part. The closing stages of the year are likely to be a particularly pleasing time for him, with October being a significant month.

This will be a favourable year for the *Water Monkey*. In addition to obtaining much satisfaction from his many interests, he can also look forward to some most enjoyable times with his family and friends. Both domestically and socially 1995 will be a very satisfying year for him. However, to maximize the favourable trends that prevail, the Water Monkey would do well to decide upon his priorities for the year and set himself some objectives to aim for. These can concern almost any aspect of his life, from moving, changing the nature of his work or achieving a personal ambition to taking up a new interest, but by having something specific to aim for he will find that he will be able to make more effective use of his time as well as concentrating his efforts towards his objective. In all that he does, however, the Water Monkey should resist the temptation of rushing decisions or taking action on the spur of the moment. Time is on his side and by thoughtful and careful planning the Water Monkey will be able to achieve much over the year. He will also be helped by the support of those around him and would do well to listen carefully to the views and advice he is given. He will enjoy the travelling that he undertakes over the year and a holiday taken in the late summer will prove both enjoyable and beneficial for him. He will also be fortunate in financial matters, although it would still be in his interests to keep a close watch on his level of outgoings. Generally, 1995 will be a positive year for the Water Monkey and by planning his activities carefully, he will experience many satisfying and rewarding moments.

If, in recent years, the *Wood Monkey* has not made the progress he would have liked or has experienced any sadness or set-backs in his life, 1995 will mark a distinct improvement in his fortunes. He should view the year as the start of a new chapter in his life. It is a time when he should be bold and enterprising and follow up any opportunities that he sees. Whether he wants a new job, promotion, new friends or has some personal ambition he wishes to fulfil, much is possible over the year. However, in order to make progress, he will need to act and take the initiative. With a positive and determined attitude, the Wood Monkey can achieve much. He will also see an improvement in his financial situation and, if his position allows, he would do well to set a regular sum aside for something specific, such as a holiday or something special he wishes to buy for himself or his home. He will be surprised at how much he can accumulate in a reasonably short time. The Wood Monkey will enjoy the travelling that he undertakes over the year, especially any short breaks. His family and friends will also be a great source of pleasure to him, although he may have to assist a close relation or friend who has some difficulty to overcome; the advice and support he is able to give will be much appreciated. Also, if he himself has any matter that is troubling him, he should not hesitate to seek the opinions of those around him. His family and friends will be keen to assist him and he will be reassured and encouraged by the support he is given. Generally, 1995 will be a positive and fulfilling year for the Wood Monkey and it rests with him to decide upon and pursue his objectives in his usual characteristic and determined manner.

This will be a positive and fulfilling year for the *Fire Monkey*. If he is seeking work, promotion or a change in his career, he should remain alert for opportunities and openings to pursue. By remaining vigilant and taking positive action, his progress and achievements in 1995 can be truly significant. Many Fire Monkeys will find themselves in a greatly improved position by the end of the year. Those who are involved in commerce are likely to do especially well. Financial matters are also favourably aspected. The Fire Monkey's domestic life is likely to keep him busy and he will be able to take great delight in the successes enjoyed by someone very close to him. His social life will also bring him much happiness, particularly over the summer months. However, while 1995 will be a generally good year for the Fire Monkey, he may have to overcome several problems. These could involve a bureaucratic matter or maybe a difference of opinion with someone; in either case the Fire Monkey would do well to resolve matters as quickly and effectively as he can rather than allow it to linger in the background. Also, for all his considerable talents, the Fire Monkey can sometimes be over-ambitious and he should be wary of committing himself to too many undertakings all at the same time. If he does, he could find he is spreading his energies too widely and not making the most of his talents. Throughout the year he will find it helpful to plan his various activities and commitments and at busy times make sure he gives himself priorities. Good organization will lead to far better and more satisfying results. The Fire Monkey will greatly enjoy any holidays that he takes over the year, especially if he visits areas that are new to him or which appeal to his sense of the unusual.

This will be a fulfilling and rewarding year for the *Earth Monkey*. Admittedly not all his plans may work out in the manner he would like, but providing he is prepared to be flexible in his attitude and adjust to new situations as they arise he can do well. He can make considerable progress in his career and if he is seeking employment or a new position he will find that his perseverance will be rewarded. He will also be successful in money matters, although he would still be advised not to get involved in any risky or speculative ventures. If he enters into any large transaction over the year he should also make sure that he is aware of all the implications involved. His family and friends will, however, be a great source of pleasure to him and his domestic life will contain many happy moments. Those around him will be most supportive and he can also look forward to attending several memorable social functions over the year. For those Earth Monkeys who are unattached or who may have had some sadness in recent years, 1995 will be a year of new opportunities and new friends. The Earth Monkey's social life will certainly be busier than it has been in recent times. However, as this will be an active year for him, it is important that he sets a regular time aside to relax and to devote to recreational activities. If he is tempted to overdo things, he could end up feeling tired as well as leaving himself prone to minor ailments. Generally, however, 1995 will be a positive and rewarding year for the Earth Monkey and for those who are prepared to seek out opportunities in which to progress, the rewards of the year can be quite considerable.

FAMOUS MONKEYS

Michael Aspel, Mike Atherton, George Baker, Bobby Ball, J. M. Barrie, David Bellamy, Jacqueline Bisset, Bjorn Borg, Frank Bough, Faith Brown, Yul Brynner, Julius Caesar, Marti Caine, Princess Caroline of Monaco, Johnny Cash, Roy Castle, Chelsea Clinton, John Constable, Alistair Cooke, Joan Crawford, Charles Dickens, Jonathan Dimbleby, Jason Donovan, Kenny Everett, Mia Farrow, Michael Fish, F. Scott Fitzgerald, Ian Fleming, Dick Francis, Paul Gauguin, Jerry Hall, Tom Hanks, Roy Hattersley, Stephen Hendry, Patricia Highsmith, Harry Houdini, Tony Jacklin, P. D. James, Pope John Paul II, Lyndon B. Johnson, Edward Kennedy, Nigel Kennedy, Jonathan King, Gladys Knight, Lord Lawson, Leo McKern, Walter Matthau, Princess Michael of Kent, Kylie Minogue, Martina Navratilova, Jack Nicklaus, Derek Nimmo, Peter O'Toole, Chris Patten, Robert Powell, Mario Puzo, Debbie Reynolds, Tim Rice, Little Richard, Angela Rippon, Diana Ross, Tom Selleck, Omar Sharif, Wilbur Smith, Koo Stark, Rod Stewart, Michael Stich, Elizabeth Taylor, Graham Taylor, Dame Kiri Te Kanawa, Harry Truman, Leonardo da Vinci, Brian Walden, the Duchess of Windsor, Bobby Womack.

22 JANUARY 1909 ～ 9 FEBRUARY 1910   *Earth Rooster*

8 FEBRUARY 1921 ～ 27 JANUARY 1922   *Metal Rooster*

26 JANUARY 1933 ～ 13 FEBRUARY 1934   *Water Rooster*

13 FEBRUARY 1945 ～ 1 FEBRUARY 1946   *Wood Rooster*

31 JANUARY 1957 ～ 17 FEBRUARY 1958   *Fire Rooster*

17 FEBRUARY 1969 ～ 5 FEBRUARY 1970   *Earth Rooster*

5 FEBRUARY 1981 ～ 24 JANUARY 1982   *Metal Rooster*

23 JANUARY 1993 ～ 9 FEBRUARY 1994   *Water Rooster*

THE
ROOSTER

THE PERSONALITY OF THE ROOSTER

A reputation for good judgement, for fair dealing, for
truth, and for rectitude, is itself a fortune.
— *Henry Ward Beecher: a Rooster*

The Rooster is born under the sign of candour. He has a
flamboyant and colourful personality and is meticulous in
all that he does. He is an excellent organizer and wherever
possible likes to plan his various activities well in advance.

The Rooster is highly intelligent and usually very well
read. He has a good sense of humour and is an effective
and persuasive speaker. He loves discussion and enjoys
taking part in any sort of debate. He has no hesitation in
speaking his mind and is forthright in his views. He does,
however, lack tact and can easily damage his reputation or
cause offence by some thoughtless remark or action. The
Rooster also has a very volatile nature and he should
always try to avoid acting on the spur of the moment.

The Rooster is usually very dignified in his manner and
conducts himself with an air of confidence and authority.
He is adept at handling financial matters and, as with most
things, he organizes his financial affairs with considerable
skill. He chooses his investments well and is capable of
achieving great wealth. Most Roosters save or use their
money wisely, but there are a few who are the reverse and
are notorious spendthrifts. Fortunately, the Rooster has
great earning capacity and is rarely without sufficient
funds to tide himself over.

Another characteristic of the Rooster is that he invariably carries a notebook or scraps of paper around with him. He is constantly writing himself reminders or noting down important facts lest he forgets – the Rooster cannot abide inefficiency and conducts all his activities in an orderly, precise and methodical manner.

The Rooster is usually very ambitious, but can be unrealistic in some of the things that he hopes to achieve. He occasionally lets his imagination run away with him and, while he does not like any interference in the things that he does, it would be in his own interests if he were to listen to the views of others a little more often. He also does not like criticism and if he feels anybody is doubting his judgement or prying too closely into his affairs, the Rooster is certain to let his feelings be known. He can also be rather self-centred and stubborn over relatively trivial matters, but to compensate for this he is reliable, honest and trustworthy, and this is very much appreciated by all who come into contact with him.

Roosters born between the hours of five and seven (both at dawn and sundown) tend to be the most extrovert of their sign, but all Roosters like to lead an active social life and enjoy attending parties and big functions. The Rooster usually has a wide circle of friends and is able to build up influential contacts with remarkable ease. He often belongs to several clubs and societies and involves himself in a variety of different activities. He is particularly interested in the environment, humanitarian affairs and anything affecting the welfare of others. The Rooster has a very caring nature and will do much to help those less fortunate than himself.

He also gets much pleasure from gardening and, while

he may not always spend as much time in the garden as he would like, his garden is invariably well-kept and extremely productive.

The Rooster is generally very distinguished in his appearance and, if his job permits, he will wear an official uniform with great pride and dignity. He is not averse to publicity and takes great delight in being the centre of attention. He often does well at PR work or any job which brings him into contact with the media. He also makes a very good teacher.

The lady Rooster leads a varied and interesting life. She involves herself in many different activities and there are some who wonder how she can achieve so much. The lady Rooster often holds very strong views and, like her male counterpart, has no hesitation in speaking her mind or telling others how she thinks things should be done. She is supremely efficient and well-organized and her home is usually very neat and tidy. The lady Rooster has good taste in clothes and usually wears smart but very practical outfits.

The Rooster usually has a large family and as a parent takes a particularly active interest in the education of his children. He is very loyal to his partner and will find that he is especially well-suited to those born under the signs of the Snake, Horse, Ox and Dragon. Provided they do not interfere too much in the Rooster's various activities, the Rat, Tiger, Goat and Pig can also establish a good relationship with the Rooster, but two Roosters together are likely to squabble and irritate each other. The rather sensitive Rabbit will find the Rooster a bit too blunt for his liking, and the Rooster will quickly become exasperated by the ever-inquisitive and artful Monkey. The Rooster will also find it difficult to get on with the Dog.

If the Rooster can overcome his volatile nature and exercise more tact in some of the things that he says, he will go far in life. He is capable and talented and will invariably make a lasting – and usually favourable – impression almost everywhere he goes.

THE FIVE DIFFERENT TYPES OF ROOSTER

In addition to the 12 signs of the Chinese zodiac, there are five elements and these have a strengthening or moderating influence on the sign. The effects of the five elements on the Rooster are described below, together with the years in which the elements were exercising their influence. Therefore all Roosters born in 1921 and 1981 are Metal Roosters, those born in 1933 and 1993 are Water Roosters, and so on.

Metal Rooster: 1921, 1981

The Metal Rooster is a hard and conscientious worker. He knows exactly what he wants in life and sets about everything he does in a positive and determined manner. He can at times appear abrasive and he would almost certainly do better if he were more willing to reach a compromise with others rather than hold so rigidly to his firmly held beliefs. He is very articulate and most astute when dealing with financial matters. He is loyal to his friends and often devotes much energy to working for the common good.

Water Rooster: 1933, 1993

This Rooster has a very persuasive manner and can easily gain the co-operation of others. He is intelligent, well-read, and gets much enjoyment from taking part in discussions and debates. He has a seemingly inexhaustible amount of energy and is prepared to work long hours in order to secure what he wants. He can, however, waste much valuable time worrying over minor and inconsequential details. He is approachable, has a good sense of humour and is highly regarded by others.

Wood Rooster: 1945

The Wood Rooster is honest, reliable and often sets himself high standards. He is ambitious, but also more prepared to work in a team than some of the other types of Rooster. He usually succeeds in life but does have a tendency to get caught up in bureaucratic matters or attempt too many things all at the same time. He has wide interests, likes to travel, and is very considerate and caring towards his family and friends.

Fire Rooster: 1897, 1957

This Rooster is extremely strong-willed. He has many leadership qualities, is an excellent organizer and is most efficient in his work. Through sheer force of character he often secures his objectives, but he does have a tendency to be very forthright and not always consider the feelings of others. If the Fire Rooster can learn to be more tactful he can often succeed beyond his wildest dreams.

Earth Rooster: 1909, 1969

This Rooster has a deep and penetrating mind. He is extremely efficient, very perceptive, and is particularly astute in business and financial matters. He is also persistent and once he has set himself an objective, he will rarely allow himself to be deflected from achieving his aim. The Earth Rooster works hard and is held in great esteem by his friends and colleagues. He usually gets much enjoyment from the arts and takes a keen interest in the activities of the various members of his family.

PROSPECTS FOR THE ROOSTER IN 1995

The Chinese New Year starts on 31 January 1995. Until then, the old year, the Year of the Dog, is still making its presence felt.

The Year of the Dog (10 February 1994 to 30 January 1995) will have been a variable year for the Rooster. Although he will have made progress in some of his activities, this will not have been without considerable effort on his part. He could also have had to overcome some difficulties over the year and found that some of his plans have not worked out in the manner he would have liked.

For what remains of the Dog year the Rooster still needs

to exercise caution with many of his activities. This is just not a time when he can take risks or be over-ambitious in his activities. Indeed, to obtain best results the Rooster would do well to concentrate on specific objectives, preferably in areas in which he has experience. If, however, he is able to add to his skills at this time or give some thought to his future – particularly his career – he will find that this will be of considerable help to him in the new year. From November 1994 the Rooster will notice a gradual upturn in his fortunes and this will carry on through to the next year. It is therefore in the Rooster's best interests to be prepared for this improvement!

The Rooster does, however, need to be careful in financial matters in the closing stages of the year and he should keep a close eye on his level of expenditure. Without care he could find that he has been spending more than he thought and this could cause him problems later. On a more positive note, he will have some enjoyable times with his family and friends and for those Roosters who are seeking friends or unattached, the aspects for romance and establishing new friendships are most encouraging. December 1994 and the first few months of 1995 will be a particularly auspicious time. There will also be opportunities for the Rooster to travel towards the end of the Dog year and his journeys are likely to prove most pleasurable, especially if they are to see friends or relations he has not seen for some time.

The Year of the Pig starts on 31 January. This will be a favourable year for the Rooster and he will now be able to make the progress that may have been eluding him in recent times. Indeed, the Rooster himself will begin to feel more enthusiastic in his outlook and will set about his activities with a renewed sense of optimism, determined to make the most of his many abilities.

In his work and career the aspects are most encouraging. The experience he has gained in recent years will now be rewarded and if he is seeking promotion or a more responsible position, he should make every effort to follow up any openings that he sees. Many Roosters will be given increased responsibilities or change the nature of their work this year and there will be several excellent opportunities to pursue. Those Roosters who are seeking work should continue to follow up any vacancies that interest them and while there may be some set-backs and disappointments in their quest for work, many will be fortunate in securing a new position, possibly at a moment when they least expect it! However, while career matters will generally go well, should the Rooster experience any difficulties or problems in his work over the year, he should regard these as challenges to overcome and triumph over. He should remember that out of challenges and set-backs often arise new and sometimes better opportunities and there will certainly be plenty of opportunities for him to pursue over the year.

The Rooster will also see an improvement in his financial situation. However, he would still do well to keep a close watch over his level of expenditure and to check carefully the terms of any large transaction he enters into. He should be particularly careful if he intends to spend a sizeable amount on the spur of the moment. This is a year for caution and prudence. Providing he bears this in mind, however, the Rooster's financial situation will steadily improve over the year.

There is one other area where he does need to exercise care and this is when dealing with any matter concerning his accommodation or property. If the Rooster is thinking of moving over the year he should make sure that he is satisfied with all aspects of the transaction and that the paperwork is in order. On no account should he allow himself to be hurried into taking any action against his better judgement. Alternatively, if he intends to have any alterations carried out on his property, either by himself or others, he should make sure he has planned and costed the work carefully. While the Rooster is by nature very thorough and methodical, without care property matters could cause him problems over the year.

The Rooster can, however, look forward to an active and enjoyable social life. He will attend some memorable social functions in 1995 – particularly in the summer – and he will extend his circle of friends and acquaintances quite considerably. This is also a good year for those Roosters who are unattached. Romance is well aspected and June and July could be especially happy and meaningful months.

The Rooster's family life will also give him much pleasure. Those around him will be most supportive and he would do well to involve his family in his various activities. Those Roosters who may have been experiencing strains in some of their relationships will find that these are likely to ease during the year. If the Rooster feels that he still has a problem in his relations with someone, be it family or friend, he should look at the cause and see if an amicable solution can be found. By addressing the matter in a sensible and conciliatory manner, he will do much to heal any disagreements or differences that may have arisen. Personal relationships are generally well aspected over the year and both his family and social life will give the Rooster much pleasure.

As this will be quite a busy year for the Rooster, he may find that he does not have as much time to devote to his hobbies and interests as he would like. However, despite the many demands on him, he should still make sure that he sets a regular time aside for recreational pursuits, especially those that give him a change from his everyday activities. If he has recently taken up a new hobby or skill, he should persist with it, even though he might be tempted to abandon it. In years to come he will be grateful that he made the effort to continue what he has started. If the Rooster does not get much exercise during the day, he would also do well to consider doing some extra walking or some other physical activity. Anything positive that he can do to improve his fitness and well-being will not only make him feel better in himself but enable him to enjoy the year that much more.

Generally, 1995 will be a positive year for the Rooster. There will be opportunities to pursue, particularly in his work, and many areas of his life will give him pleasure and satisfaction. His social and domestic life will be enjoyable and he will also be able to extend his circle of friends and acquaintances. However, most significantly over the year, the Rooster will feel more determined to make the most of his considerable abilities and talents. He will feel more optimistic and enthusiastic than he may have done in recent times and this new and positive attitude will guide him to some worthy accomplishments over the year.

As far as the different types of Rooster are concerned, 1995 will be an important year for the *Metal Rooster*. He can make pleasing progress in many of his activities and can achieve a great deal over the year. However, to make the most of these generally favourable trends, he would do well to decide what his priorities are for the year. With some plan or objective in mind – and the Metal Rooster is usually good at planning ahead – he will then be able to concentrate his efforts on something specific and also be in a better position to take advantage of the opportunities that will occur over the year. Those Metal Roosters involved in academic work will do particularly well and, in addition to their current progress, they should give some thought to their future. If possible, they should talk to those with experience and seek advice and guidance. In this way, the Metal Rooster will not only accomplish much in 1995 but prepare the way for progress in future years. He will also obtain much satisfaction from his hobbies. Travel and outdoor activities are especially well aspected. Financial matters will generally go well, but the Metal Rooster does still need to keep a careful check on his outgoings. Like all Roosters, he needs to be particularly careful if he is involved in any transactions concerning property, especially if he intends to move over the year. If he has any doubts over matters to do with his property or accommodation, he would do well to seek professional advice. He will, however, lead a most pleasant social life over the year and, for the unattached Metal Rooster, romance is very well aspected. The Metal Rooster's domestic life will also be pleasurable, although he would do well to involve those around him in his activities and to listen closely to any advice they give him. Although he may not agree with all they say, he should remember that they have his best interests at heart and are keen to help, support and encourage him. Generally, 1995 will be a positive and fulfilling year for the Metal Rooster and by setting about his activities in his usual diligent way he will be able to achieve much over the year as well as having some most enjoyable times.

The Year of the Pig will be a significant year for the *Water Rooster*. Over the year several changes will take place and these will have an important bearing on this and the next few years. Many Water Roosters will change the nature of their work during 1995. Some will take on increased responsibilities, while others will consider retiring and devoting more time to their interests and their loved ones. In either case, the Water Rooster will be pleased with any decisions and actions that he takes. Those around him will be most supportive and at all times the Water Rooster would do well to share his thoughts and feelings with others. He will be considerably heartened by the advice and encouragement he is given and also by the considerable esteem and affection shown to him. Some Water Roosters will also move during the year; those that do should make sure that they are satisfied with all aspects of the transaction before going ahead. Property and accommodation matters do need careful attention in 1995. The Water Rooster could also see several changes in his family over the year, possibly the birth of a grandchild or the marriage of a close relation. This is very much a year of change for the Water Rooster and some of the changes will open up new opportunities for him and mark the start of a new and positive phase in his life. It is also a favourable time for putting into practice any ideas that he has or realizing a long-held ambition. If there has been a subject that has been intriguing him, now is the time to find out more or, if he has been promising himself a special holiday, this is the time to plan. By acting positively and going after his objectives, no matter what they are, the Water Rooster can turn 1995 into a memorable and satisfying year.

This will be a busy year for the *Wood Rooster*. He will be much in demand with his family and friends and can look forward to some most enjoyable times with those around him. He could also have good reason to be involved in a personal or family celebration and the year will contain several memorable events. He will also do well in his work and many Wood Roosters will be successful in obtaining a new position, taking on increased responsibilities or changing their duties. While some of the changes may at first seem daunting, the Wood Rooster is often at his best when facing new challenges and this year will be no exception. The year holds many exciting possibilities for him and it is in his interests to give of his best, to promote himself and actively pursue the opportunities that he sees. The bold and enterprising Wood Rooster can make great progress over the year. Financial matters will also go well and many Wood Roosters will see an improvement in their financial situation. On a more cautionary note, however, the Wood Rooster needs to be careful when dealing with property matters and if he intends to undertake any hazardous or strenuous activity, he must make sure he follows all the safety procedures and particularly seek help when lifting heavy objects. Throughout the year he should remember the maxim, 'It is better to be safe than sorry.' As this will be quite an active year for him, it is important that he does not neglect his own well-being. He would do well to set some regular time aside for recreational pursuits and give himself the opportunity to rest and unwind. He should also try to make sure that he takes at least one good holiday over the year and, if possible, to visit an area he has not been to before. He could find his travels will prove both enjoyable and most beneficial for him.

This can be a year of considerable potential for the *Fire Rooster*. However, his degree of success is heavily dependent on his own attitude. To make progress and maximize the favourable trends that exist, he needs to have some idea of his objectives and to concentrate his efforts on these. Careful planning and determined action will lead to some very pleasing results. The Fire Rooster would also be helped by discussing his plans with others and paying careful attention to all that is going on around him. Sometimes, usually because he gets so involved in his own activities, he does not always fully consult with others or take sufficient notice of what is happening around him. Such an attitude could work against him over the year. He will, in any case, find his progress far easier by co-operating and working with others rather than relying on his own efforts. The early part of the year is, however, likely to be a particularly significant time and many Fire Roosters will make some pleasing progress in their work at this time. The Fire Rooster will also obtain much pleasure from both his domestic and social life and can look forward to many happy family and social occasions throughout the year. His personal relationships will generally go very well for him but there is still a chance that he could find himself in disagreement with someone over the year. If such a situation arises, the Fire Rooster would do well to seek a solution to the problem as quickly as he can. If not, he could find that the disagreement could escalate and mar what will otherwise be a pleasing year for him. He is, however, likely to see an improvement in his financial position and there will also be several opportunities for him to travel over the year.

This will be a busy and rewarding year for the *Earth Rooster*. By continuing to set about his activities in his usual conscientious manner he will make considerable progress, particularly in his career. Early in the year there will be an opportunity to take on new responsibilities or change to a different type of work and the Earth Rooster is likely to find that this will give him an added incentive to do well and enable him to extend his skills and experience. Those Earth Roosters who are seeking work or unhappy in their present position should actively pursue any openings that they see – a persistent approach will lead to positive results. The Earth Rooster will do well in financial matters and if he has been experiencing financial problems he will find these will ease during the year. He could also find it helpful to conduct a review of his current outgoings and to make any changes he feels necessary – he could be surprised at the difference this makes! The Earth Rooster's personal and domestic life is likely to be a great source of pleasure to him. Those around him will be supportive and encouraging and he can look forward to some very happy family occasions. Many Earth Roosters will see an addition to their family over the year or take particular delight in the achievements and successes of younger relations. The year is also likely to prove memorable for the unattached Earth Rooster. His social life will be most enjoyable and romance is particularly well aspected. However, as 1995 will be a busy year for him, there could be a temptation for him to neglect some of his interests or hobbies. If possible, he should try not to let this happen. His interests will help take his mind off everyday matters and be a valuable source of relaxation for him. He will also obtain much enjoyment from any travelling that he undertakes over the year, especially to locations which appeal to his sense of adventure.

FAMOUS ROOSTERS

Kate Adie, Danny Baker, Dame Janet Baker, Severiano Ballesteros, Michael Bentine, Lloyd Bentsen, Sir Dirk Bogarde, Barbara Taylor Bradford, Julian Bream, Richard Briers, Michael Caine, Jasper Carrott, Enrico Caruso, Charles Cazenove, Jean Chrétien, Eric Clapton, Joan Collins, Rita Coolidge, Dickie Davies, Steve Davis, Deanna Durbin, the Duke of Edinburgh, Gloria Estefan, Douglas Fairbanks Jnr., Nick Faldo, Bryan Ferry, Errol Flynn, Stephen Fry, Steffi Graf, Richard Harris, Deborah Harry, Goldie Hawn, Katherine Hepburn, James Herbert, Michael Heseltine, Diane Keaton, Dean Koontz, Bernhard Langer, D. H. Lawrence, Martyn Lewis, David Livingstone, Ken Livingstone, David McCallum, Jayne Mansfield, Steve Martin, James Mason, W. Somerset Maugham, Bette Middler, Van Morrison, Paul Nicholas, Barry Norman, Kim Novak, Yoko Ono, Donny Osmond, Dolly Parton, Michelle Pfeiffer, Roman Polanski, Priscilla Presley, Nancy Reagan, Joan Rivers, Bobby Robson, Sir Harry Secombe, George Segal, Carly Simon, Johann Strauss, Jacqueline Susann, Jayne Torvill, Sir Peter Ustinov, Richard Wagner.

10 FEBRUARY 1910 ～ 29 JANUARY 1911	*Metal Dog*
28 JANUARY 1922 ～ 15 FEBRUARY 1923	*Water Dog*
14 FEBRUARY 1934 ～ 3 FEBRUARY 1935	*Wood Dog*
2 FEBRUARY 1946 ～ 21 JANUARY 1947	*Fire Dog*
18 FEBRUARY 1958 ～ 7 FEBRUARY 1959	*Earth Dog*
6 FEBRUARY 1970 ～ 26 JANUARY 1971	*Metal Dog*
25 JANUARY 1982 ～ 12 FEBRUARY 1983	*Water Dog*
10 FEBRUARY 1994 ～ 30 JANUARY 1995	*Wood Dog*

THE
DOG

THE PERSONALITY OF THE DOG

If you think you can win, you can win. Faith is necessary
to victory.

— William Hazlitt: a Dog

The Dog is born under the signs of loyalty and anxiety. He
usually holds very firm views and beliefs and is the cham-
pion of good causes. He hates any sort of injustice or unfair
treatment and will do all in his power to help those less
fortunate than himself. He has a strong sense of fair play
and will be honourable and open in all his dealings.

The Dog is very direct and straightforward. He is never
one to skirt round issues and speaks frankly and to the
point. He can also be stubborn, but he is more than
prepared to listen to the views of others and will try to be
as fair as possible in coming to his decisions. He will
readily give advice where it is needed and will be the first
to offer assistance when things go wrong.

The Dog instils confidence wherever he goes and there
are many who admire him for his integrity and resolute
manner. He is a very good judge of character and he can
often form an accurate impression of someone very shortly
after meeting them. He is also very intuitive and can
frequently sense how things are going to work out.

Despite his friendly and amiable manner, the Dog is not
a big socializer. He dislikes having to attend large social
functions or parties and much prefers a quiet meal with
friends or a chat by the fire. The Dog is an excellent
conversationalist and is often a marvellous raconteur of
amusing stories and anecdotes.

He is also quick-witted and his mind is always alert. He can keep calm in a crisis and although he does have a temper, his outbursts tend to be short-lived. The Dog is loyal and trustworthy, but if he ever feels badly let down or rejected by someone, he will rarely forgive or forget.

The Dog usually has very set interests. He prefers to specialize and become an expert in a chosen area rather than dabble in a variety of different activities. He usually does well in jobs where he feels that he is being of service to others and is often suited to careers in the social services, the medical and legal professions and teaching. The Dog does, however, need to feel motivated in his work. He has to have a sense of purpose in the things that he does and if ever this is lacking he can quite often drift through life without ever achieving very much. Once he has the motivation, however, very little can prevent him from securing his objective.

Another characteristic of the Dog is his tendency to worry and to view things rather pessimistically. Quite often these worries are totally unnecessary and are of his own making. Although it may be difficult, worrying is a habit which the Dog should try to overcome.

The Dog is not materialistic or particularly bothered about accumulating great wealth. As long as he has the necessary money to support his family and to spend on the occasional luxury, he is more than happy. However, when he does have any spare money the Dog tends to be rather a spendthrift and does not always put his money to its best use. He is also not a very good speculator and would be advised to get professional advice before entering into any major long-term investment.

The Dog will rarely be short of admirers, but he is not an easy person to live with. His moods are changeable and his standards high, but he will be loyal and protective to his partner and will do all in his power to provide her with a good and comfortable home. He can get on extremely well with those born under the signs of the Horse, Pig, Tiger and Monkey, and can also establish a sound and stable relationship with the Rat, Ox, Rabbit, Snake and another Dog, but will find the Dragon a bit too flamboyant for his liking. He will also find it difficult to understand the creative and imaginative Goat and is likely to be highly irritated by the candid Rooster.

The female Dog is renowned for her beauty. She has a warm and caring nature, although until she knows someone well she can be both secretive and very guarded. She is highly intelligent and despite her calm and tranquil appearance she can be extremely ambitious. She enjoys sport and other outdoor activities and has a happy knack of finding bargains in the most unlikely of places. The female Dog can also get rather impatient when things do not work out as she would like.

The Dog usually has a very good way with children and can be a loving and doting parent.

The Dog will rarely be happier than when he is helping someone or doing something that will benefit others. Providing he can cure himself of his tendency to worry, he will lead a very full and active life – and in that life he will make many friends and do a tremendous amount of good.

THE FIVE DIFFERENT TYPES OF DOG

In addition to the 12 signs of the Chinese zodiac, there are five elements and these have a strengthening or moderating influence on the sign. The effects of the five elements on the Dog are described below, together with the years in which the elements were exercising their influence. Therefore all Dogs born in 1910 and 1970 are Metal Dogs, those born in 1922 and 1982 are Water Dogs, and so on.

Metal Dog: 1910, 1970
The Metal Dog is bold, confident and forthright, and sets about everything he does in a resolute and determined manner. He has a great belief in his abilities and has no hesitation about speaking his mind or devoting himself to some just cause. He can be rather serious at times and can get anxious and irritable when things are not going according to plan. He tends to have very specific interests and it would certainly help him to broaden his outlook and also become more involved in group activities. He is extremely loyal and faithful to his friends.

Water Dog: 1922, 1982
The Water Dog has a very direct and outgoing personality. He is an excellent communicator and has little trouble in persuading others to fall in with his plans. He does, however, have a somewhat carefree nature and is not as disciplined or as thorough as he should be in certain

matters. Neither does he keep as much control over his finances as he should, but he can be most generous to his family and friends and will make sure that they want for nothing. The Water Dog is usually very good with children and has a wide circle of friends.

Wood Dog: 1934, 1994

This Dog is a hard and conscientious worker and will usually make a favourable impression wherever he goes. He is less independent than some of the other types of Dog and prefers to work in a group rather than on his own. He is popular, has a good sense of humour, and takes a very keen interest in the activities of the various members of his family. He is often attracted to the finer things in life and can get much pleasure from collecting stamps, coins, pictures or antiques. He also prefers to live in the country rather than the town.

Fire Dog: 1946

This Dog has a lively, outgoing personality and is able to establish friendships with remarkable ease. He is an honest and conscientious worker and likes to take an active part in all that is going on around him. He also likes to explore new ideas and, providing he can get the necessary support and advice, he can often succeed where others have failed. He does, however, have a tendency to be stubborn. Providing he can overcome this, the Fire Dog can often achieve considerable fame and fortune.

Earth Dog: 1898, 1958

The Earth Dog is very talented and astute. He is methodical and efficient and is capable of going far in his chosen profession. He tends to be rather quiet and reserved but has a very persuasive manner and usually secures his objectives without too much opposition. He is generous and kind and is always ready to lend a helping hand when it is needed. He is also held in very high esteem by his friends and colleagues and he is usually most dignified in his appearance.

PROSPECTS FOR THE DOG IN 1995

The Chinese New Year starts on 31 January 1995. Until then, the old year, the Year of the Dog, is still making its presence felt.

The Year of the Dog (10 February 1994 to 30 January 1995) is a highly favourable year for the Dog and the closing months of the year are particularly well aspected. The Dog will be able to accomplish much and should do all he can to promote and pursue his interests. If he is seeking work or a change in work, he should follow up any opportunities that he sees or, if he has some personal project he wishes to develop, now would be a good time to act. Similarly, if he wishes to change his accommodation or have some improvements carried out to his property, he should make enquiries and consider putting his plans in motion at this time. In order to take advantage of these favourable trends, however, the Dog must remain positive, determined and prepared to act. If he just rests on past and present achievements he could miss some wonderful opportunities. By asserting himself, going after his goals and by taking positive action, however, he will soon begin to see pleasing results. Even if he feels that he has not made as much use of the auspicious trends as he could over the year, it is not too late to put this into practice. For many Dogs, the Dog year will be the start of a positive phase in life and their efforts and the experience they gain will serve them well in the new Chinese year.

Also, the Dog's domestic and social life is likely to be most pleasurable at this time. His family and friends will be supportive and can give him much useful encouragement and advice. He will also attend several enjoyable social functions towards the end of the year and many Dogs will see a noticeable upturn in their social life. The Dog would do well to remain alert to all that is going on around him in December 1994 and January 1995. By doing so, he could learn some information which will be of great value to him in the year ahead.

The Year of the Pig starts on 31 January and is going to be a pleasing year for the Dog. He will be able to build on the achievements of last year and will make continued progress. Many of his activities will go well and the year will also contain some very enjoyable times for him.

Domestically and socially, this will be a most fulfilling year. The Dog's domestic life will be settled and content and he can look forward to having some memorable times with his loved ones. He will also find it helpful to discuss his hopes, plans and aspirations with those around him, particularly in the early stages of the Pig year. Their advice will be most helpful and throughout the year the Dog will be reassured by the support and encouragement he is given.

The Dog is likely to undertake a number of improvements to his home and garden over the year and these should go well. However, in all his domestic undertakings he should make sure that he involves his family in what he does. He will be grateful for the assistance they are able to give and will find that joint activities will not only be mutually satisfying but give those involved a greater sense of achievement.

The Dog's social life will also be pleasant and he can look forward to attending several enjoyable social events over the year, especially in the spring months. Any Dog who feels lonely or would like more friends should make every effort to go out more and get in contact with others. They will be pleased they have made the effort and will find that positive action on their part will bring results.

One trait of the Dog, though, is his tendency to worry. So while, as in every year, there will be problems to face and overcome, he should try not to let them mar what will be a good year for him. If troubled by any matter, he should not hesitate to seek the advice of those around him – his family and friends are there to help and assist him, and he will find that they will provide valuable assistance if he asks. It is also likely that the Dog will himself assist someone close to him who has some difficult matter to overcome and the support he is able to give will be much appreciated. Others value his sterling qualities, particularly his sincerity and understanding nature.

There will also be opportunities for the Dog to make progress in his work over the year and he should make every effort to advance his plans and ideas. If he sees any openings or vacancies that he wishes to pursue, he should not hesitate to follow these up. By remaining persistent and bringing his skills and talents to the attention of others, he can make substantial progress. The Dog should also use any opportunities that he gets to go on courses, to obtain further skills or widen his experience. By doing so he will do much to enhance his prospects, both in the latter part of this year and in the next few years. March, June and October could be significant months for work opportunities and the Dog would do well to remain alert for openings to pursue then.

The Dog can also look forward to some financial good fortune over the year and many Dogs will see a significant improvement in their financial situation. Any investments that the Dog is able to make for his longer-term future could build into a useful asset in years to come. His luck could also extend to being successful in competitions and if he sees any that interest him, it would be worth his entering. Virtually all Dogs will enjoy some surprises over the year and winning a competition could be one of them!

The Dog will enjoy any holidays or breaks that he takes in 1995, although he does need to be careful when making travel arrangements. Without proper planning he could find some journeys will prove difficult and mar what will otherwise be an enjoyable time away.

As this will be quite a busy year for the Dog, he should make sure that he sets some regular time aside for recreational pursuits, particularly those that give him a break from his usual everyday activities. It may also be worth his while to consider taking up a completely new interest, possibly something unrelated to anything he has done before. He could find the challenge this gives him will not only bring him many hours of pleasure but be intellectually stimulating as well as extending his talents in other ways. In some respects, the Year of the Pig is a year of innovation for the Dog and will be a chance for him to try something new. By seeking new interests and challenges and pursuing the opportunities the year will bring, the Dog will obtain many satisfying results. In addition to this, his family and social life will give him much happiness, making this a truly satisfying and pleasing year for him.

As far as the different types of Dog are concerned, 1995 will be a constructive and rewarding year for the *Metal Dog*. Over the year there will be several excellent opportunities for him to pursue and at all times he should remain alert to what is going on around him and follow up any openings that he sees. It would also be in his interests to be reasonably flexible in his attitude over the year. Usually the Metal Dog has very set ideas on his objectives and, while such farsightedness is admirable, in the short term it could restrict his progress. In 1995 the Metal Dog should concentrate on widening his experience and skills and be prepared to be adaptable should circumstances dictate. The knowledge and skills he is able to obtain over the year will serve him well in the future. Any Metal Dog seeking work or wanting a change in his work should again follow up any openings that he sees and possibly look at a type of work that he may not have considered before – a change could help him to widen his experience as well as enhancing his future prospects. Almost all Metal Dogs will make pleasing progress in their work in 1995. Financial matters are also well aspected and the Metal Dog is likely to see an improvement in his financial situation over the year. He could also be fortunate in several purchases that he makes, especially items for his home, and it would be in his interests to keep a keen look out for bargains in shops, particularly at sale times. Domestically, this will be a busy year for him and he will spend much of his spare time on projects around his home and in helping relations. Although there may be times when he feels tired and fraught with the demands placed upon him, his efforts will be greatly appreciated. If, however, at any time over the year he feels that too much is being asked of him, he should not hesitate to ask for assistance from his family and close friends. They will be delighted to help and will try to ease any burden he might be under. As his domestic life is likely to keep him busy, the Metal Dog could find the time he has for his interests and for socializing rather restricted. He should nevertheless make sure that he gets away for at least one holiday and that he also allows himself time to regularly unwind and relax. When times are busy, he could find walking, swimming, cycling or some other suitable activity very beneficial. For those Metal Dogs who are unattached, the prospects for romance and for making new friends are excellent and many Metal Dogs will get engaged or married over the year. While this will be a busy year, virtually all Metal Dogs will have good reason to look back on 1995 as a happy and memorable year.

This will be a pleasant and generally enjoyable year for the *Water Dog*. He will be much in demand with his family and friends and can look forward to attending several most enjoyable social functions over the year. There will also be opportunities to extend his circle of friends and acquaintances and his social life is likely to be busier than it has been in recent years. For any Water Dog who may have felt lonely or would like some additional company, this is an ideal year to go out more and perhaps join a local society or take up an interest that would bring him into contact with others. Anything constructive he can do will bring pleasing results. Similarly, if the Water Dog finds he has some spare time, he would do well to consider taking up an additional interest or hobby. He will not only find that this will give him many hours of pleasure but it could also be quite therapeutic for him. Many Water Dogs will also obtain much enjoyment from outdoor activities over the year, particularly from walking, gardening or a sporting activity. The Water Dog will enjoy any breaks or holidays that he takes, but he does need to plan his journeys and travel arrangements carefully. He will be generally fortunate in financial matters, but would do well to keep an eye on his general level of expenditure. Also, if he becomes involved in any large transaction, he should make sure he is conversant with all the terms involved. He should not allow himself to be pressurized into making any important decision (especially concerning finance) against his better judgement and, when in doubt, he would do well to seek professional advice. Those Water Dogs involved in education are likely to make pleasing progress and a new subject or skill that they begin to study now could prove of great significance in years to come.

This will be an interesting year for the *Wood Dog*. He

will be able to devote much time to his hobbies and interests and these are likely to give a considerable amount of pleasure. He could also find that an interest or skill that he has developed in recent years will prove quite lucrative for him and he would do well to get in contact with others who share similar interests. Socially, this will be an active year for him and he will build up some new and good friendships as the year progresses. He can also look forward to attending several important social functions, one of which could be an important celebration within his family. Domestic matters will go well and those around him will give him much happiness and support. However, there could still be a family matter which does give him cause for concern. Rather than keep his views to himself, he should let others know how he feels and discuss any anxieties he has. By being open in this way he will find that any problem or difference of opinion can be resolved much more easily. Fortunately, any difficulties that do arise, either in his family or in some other sphere of his life, will be short-lived and will certainly not mar what will be a favourable year for him. The Wood Dog will be fortunate in financial matters in 1995 and while some of his travel plans may not be entirely problem-free, he will very much enjoy any holidays or short breaks that he is able to take. The year will also bring about several changes for him, perhaps including a move. Generally, these changes will work out positively for him.

This will be an important and fulfilling year for the *Fire Dog*. It will contain some very happy moments for him and he will be successful in many of his undertakings. It is a year for him to be bold and positive and determined to make the best of his capabilities. With the right attitude he can make considerable progress, particularly in his work. He would do well to pursue any opportunities that he sees, advance his ideas and bring his talents to the attention of others. He should also try to take on new responsibilities over the year or consider changing to a type of work which he has not undertaken before. This will bring new and stimulating challenges for him – something which he may have felt he has been lacking in recent years. Indeed, if any Fire Dog feels that he has not been making as much progress as he could, then this is a year when he should make a concerted and determined effort to improve upon his present position. With the right attitude, this can be a year of considerable opportunity. The Fire Dog will also be fortunate in financial matters and if he has any spare money at his disposal he would do well to consider setting some aside for his longer-term future. A savings policy started now could turn into a valuable asset in years to come. The Fire Dog's family will be a great source of pride to him and he can look forward to having some most enjoyable times with his loved ones and close friends. Generally, 1995 will be a pleasant and successful year for him, although, in view of the demanding nature of the year, he should make sure he does not neglect his own well-being. He would do well to ensure he has a healthy and well-balanced diet and, if he does not get much daily exercise, to consider doing some additional and suitable activity. Some extra walking, cycling or swimming could prove most beneficial for him.

This will be an important year for the *Earth Dog*. Now he is likely to reap the rewards of his patience and efforts over recent years. Others will look favourably on his work and ideas and, providing he asserts himself and goes after his objectives, he can make considerable progress. There will be several opportunities that he can pursue in his work and many Earth Dogs will take on new duties and responsibilities over the year. Any Earth Dogs seeking work should actively pursue any openings that they see. By remaining persistent and determined they could be successful in obtaining a new position and one which could easily lead to better things in the future. The Earth Dog will lead a busy but generally enjoyable domestic and social life. He will devote much of his spare time to his family and home over the year and, while he may sometimes despair of all he has to do, the year will contain many happy times. DIY projects and home improvements will go especially well. The Earth Dog does, however, need to plan any journeys he proposes to take with care and, while he will see an improvement in his financial situation, it would still be in his interests to keep a close watch on his general level of outgoings. Without care he could find his expenditure is greater than he thought. Generally, however, 1995 will be a successful and fulfilling year for the Earth Dog and by going after his objectives and setting about his activities in his usual methodical way, he can make considerable progress. He will also find this quite a lucky year and in addition to some pleasant surprises in the summer, he could also be successful in a competition he enters.

FAMOUS DOGS

André Agassi, Kingsley Amis, Jane Asher, Brigitte Bardot, Dr Christiaan Barnard, Candice Bergman, Lionel Blair, Dr Boutros-Ghali, David Bowie, Peter Brooke, Kate Bush, Max Bygraves, King Carl Gustaf XVI of Sweden, Belinda Carlisle, Paul Cézanne, Cher, Sir Winston Churchill, Petula Clark, Bill Clinton, Leonard Cohen, Robin Cook, Henry Cooper, Jamie Lee Curtis, Timothy Dalton, Charles Dance, Christopher Dean, Claude Debussy, John Dunn, Blake Edwards, Gloria Estefan, Sally Field, Zsa Zsa Gabor, Judy Garland, Bamber Gascoigne, George Gershwin, Lenny Henry, Patricia Hodge, Victor Hugo, Barry Humphries, Michael Jackson, Henry Kelly, Felicity Kendal, Sue Lawley, Maureen Lipman, Sophia Loren, Joanna Lumley, Shirley MacLaine, Madonna, Norman Mailer, Barry Manilow, Rik Mayall, Simon Mayo, Golda Meir, Freddie Mercury, Liza Minnelli, David Niven, Gary Numan, Michelle Pfeiffer, Sydney Pollack, Elvis Presley, Priscilla Presley, Anneka Rice, Malcolm Rifkind, Paul Robeson, Linda Ronstadt, Gabriela Sabatini, Carl Sagan, Jennifer Saunders, Norman Schwarzkopf, Sylvester Stallone, Robert Louis Stevenson, David Suchet, Donald Sutherland, Chris Tarrant, Mother Teresa, Voltaire, Timothy West, Mary Whitehouse, Prince William, Ian Woosnam.

30 JANUARY 1911 ～ 17 FEBRUARY 1912	*Metal Pig*
16 FEBRUARY 1923 ～ 4 FEBRUARY 1924	*Water Pig*
4 FEBRUARY 1935 ～ 23 JANUARY 1936	*Wood Pig*
22 JANUARY 1947 ～ 9 FEBRUARY 1948	*Fire Pig*
8 FEBRUARY 1959 ～ 27 JANUARY 1960	*Earth Pig*
27 JANUARY 1971 ～ 14 FEBRUARY 1972	*Metal Pig*
13 FEBRUARY 1983 ～ 1 FEBRUARY 1984	*Water Pig*
31 JANUARY 1995 ～ 18 FEBRUARY 1996	*Wood Pig*

THE
PIG

THE PERSONALITY OF THE PIG

Sow a thought and you reap an act;
Sow an act and you reap a habit;
Sow a habit and you reap a character;
Sow a character and you reap a destiny.
                    – *Ralph Waldo Emerson: a Pig*

The Pig is born under the sign of honesty. He has a kind and understanding nature and is well-known for his abilities as a peace-maker. He hates any sort of discord or unpleasantness and will do all in his power to sort out differences of opinion or bring opposing factions together.

He is an excellent conversationalist and speaks truthfully and to the point. He dislikes any form of falsehood or hypocrisy and is a firm believer in justice and the maintenance of law and order. In spite of these beliefs, however, the Pig is reasonably tolerant and often prepared to forgive others for their wrongs. The Pig rarely harbours grudges and is never vindictive.

The Pig is usually very popular. He enjoys other people's company and likes to be involved in joint or group activities. He will be a loyal member of any club or society and can be relied upon to lend a helping hand at functions. He is also an excellent fund-raiser for charities and is often a great supporter of humanitarian causes.

The Pig is a hard and conscientious worker and is particularly respected for his reliability and integrity. In his early years he will try his hand at several different jobs, but he is usually happiest where he feels that he is being of service to others. He will unselfishly give up his time for the common good and is highly-valued by his colleagues and employers.

The Pig has a good sense of humour and invariably has a smile, joke or some whimsical remark at the ready. He loves to entertain and to please others, and there are many who have been attracted to careers in show business or who enjoy following the careers of famous stars and personalities.

There are, unfortunately, some who take advantage of the Pig's good nature and impose on his generosity. The Pig has great difficulty in saying 'no' and, although he may dislike being firm, it would be in his own interests to say occasionally, 'Enough is enough.' The Pig can also be rather naïve and gullible; however, if at any stage in his life he feels that he has been badly let down, he will make sure that it will never happen again and will try to become self-reliant. There are many Pigs who have become entrepreneurs or forged a successful career on their own after some early disappointment in life. And although the Pig tends to spend his money quite freely, he is usually very astute in financial matters and there are many Pigs who have become wealthy.

Another characteristic of the Pig is his ability to recover from set-backs reasonably quickly. His faith and his strength of character keep him going. If he thinks that there is a job he can do or has something that he wants to achieve, he will pursue it with a dogged determination. He can also be stubborn and, no matter how many may plead with him, once he has made his mind up he will rarely change his views.

Although the Pig may work hard, he also knows how to

enjoy himself. He is a great pleasure-seeker and will quite happily spend his hard-earned money on a lavish holiday or an expensive meal – for the Pig is a connoisseur of good food and wine – or take part in a variety of recreational activities. He also enjoys small social gatherings and, if he is in company he likes, the Pig can very easily become the life and soul of the party. He does, however, tend to become rather withdrawn at larger functions or when among strangers.

The Pig is also a creature of comfort and his home will usually be fitted with all the latest in luxury appliances. Where possible, he will prefer to live in the country rather than the town and will opt to have a big garden, for the Pig is usually a keen and successful gardener.

The Pig is very popular with the opposite sex and will often have numerous romances before he settles down. Once settled, however, he will be loyal and protective to his partner and he will find that he is especially well-suited to those born under the signs of the Goat, Rabbit, Dog and Tiger, and also to another Pig. Due to his affable and easy-going nature he can also establish a satisfactory relationship with all the remaining signs of the Chinese zodiac, with the exception of the Snake. The Snake tends to be wily, secretive and very guarded, and this can be intensely irritating to the honest and open-hearted Pig.

The lady Pig will devote all her energies to the needs of her children and her partner. She will try to ensure that they want for nothing and their pleasure is very much her pleasure. Her home will either be very clean and orderly or hopelessly untidy. Strangely, there seems to be no in between with the Pig – they either love housework or detest it! The lady Pig does, however, have considerable talents as an organizer and this, combined with her friendly and open manner, enables her to secure many of her objectives. She can also be a caring and conscientious parent and has very good taste in clothes.

The Pig is usually lucky in life and will rarely want for anything. Provided he does not let others take advantage of his good nature and is not afraid of asserting himself, he will go through life making friends, helping others and winning the admiration of many.

THE FIVE DIFFERENT TYPES OF PIG

In addition to the 12 signs of the Chinese zodiac, there are five elements and these have a strengthening or moderating influence on the sign. The effects of the five elements on the Pig are described below, together with the years in which the elements were exercising their influence. Therefore all Pigs born in 1911 and 1971 are Metal Pigs, those born in 1923 and 1983 are Water Pigs, and so on.

Metal Pig: 1911, 1971

The Metal Pig is more ambitious and determined than some of the other types of Pig. He is strong, energetic and likes to be involved in a wide variety of different activities. He is very open and forthright in his views, although he can be a little too trusting at times and has a tendency to accept things at face value. He has a good sense of humour and loves to attend parties and other social gatherings. He has a warm, outgoing nature and usually has a large circle of friends.

Water Pig: 1923, 1983

The Water Pig has a heart of gold. He is generous and loyal and tries to remain on good terms with everyone. He will do his utmost to help others, but sadly there are some who will take advantage of his kind nature and he should, in his own interests, be a little more discriminating and be prepared to stand firm against anything that he does not like. Although he prefers the quieter things in life, he has a wide range of interests. He particularly enjoys outdoor pursuits and attending parties and social occasions. He is a hard and conscientious worker and invariably does well in his chosen profession. He is also gifted in the art of communication.

Wood Pig: 1935, 1995

This Pig has a friendly, persuasive manner and is easily able to gain the confidence of others. He likes to be involved in all that is going on around him and can sometimes take on more responsibility than he can properly handle. He is loyal to his family and friends and he also derives much pleasure from helping those less fortunate than himself. The Wood Pig is usually an optimist and leads a very full, enjoyable and satisfying life. He also has a good sense of humour.

Fire Pig: 1947

The Fire Pig is both energetic and adventurous and he sets about everything he does in a confident and resolute manner. He is very forthright in his views and does not mind taking risks in order to achieve his objectives. He can, however, get carried away by the excitement of the moment and ought to exercise more caution with some of the enterprises in which he gets involved. The Fire Pig is usually lucky in money matters and is well known for his generosity. He is also very caring towards the members of his family.

Earth Pig: 1899, 1959

This Pig has a kindly nature. He is sensible and realistic and will go to great lengths in order to please his employers and to secure his aims and ambitions. He is an excellent organizer and is particularly astute in business and financial matters. He has a good sense of humour and a wide circle of friends. He also likes to lead an active social life, although he does sometimes have a tendency to eat and drink more than is good for him.

PROSPECTS FOR THE PIG IN 1995

The Chinese New Year starts on 31 January 1995. Until then, the old year, the Year of the Dog, is still making its presence felt.

The Year of the Dog (10 February 1994 to 30 January 1995) will have been both a varied and interesting year for the Pig. He is likely to have made progress in many of his activities and his domestic and social life will also have given him much pleasure. The closing stages of the Dog year are, however, likely to be a busy time for the Pig. He will have quite a heavy workload and will be much in demand with those around him. With so much activity going on, he should decide upon his priorities and resist the temptation to over-commit himself. Time is on his side, and provided he organizes his work and commitments well he will be pleased with just how much he can accomplish in the closing stages of the year.

The Dog year is a favourable year for the Pig to develop new skills and widen his experience and if any opportunity exists for him to add to his skills in its closing months he should do so. Anything he can do to enhance his prospects will be in his interests.

The Pig should also give some thought to his present situation and to his future, as 1995 is the Pig's own year and it is likely to be a truly auspicious one for him. However, to take advantage of these trends, he does need to have some idea of what he would like to accomplish over the next 12 months. The thought and planning that he can give to this will be time very well spent.

The Pig is likely to attend some enjoyable social functions towards the end of the Dog year and he could receive some pleasing personal news in December 1994. However, while he may be fully occupied with the festivities over the Christmas and New Year holiday, he should try to take advantage of any opportunity he gets to relax and unwind. The Year of the Dog will have been quite a demanding time for him, particularly the last few months, and by giving himself a rest, he will feel fresher, revitalized and be better able to take advantage of the exciting prospects that await him in his own year.

The Year of the Pig starts on 31 January and it will be a most rewarding and fulfilling year for the Pig. He will make considerable progress in many of his activities as well as having some enjoyable times with his family and friends.

To take advantage of the splendid trends of the year, the Pig needs to have some idea about what he wishes to attain. This could concern a personal ambition or project, his career, moving or carrying out improvements to his home. Progress is possible in all these areas but to maximize these trends and to take advantage of any opportunities that he sees, the Pig needs to set himself some goals and objectives to aim for.

He is likely to do particularly well in his work and many Pigs will move to a more responsible and rewarding position during the year. All Pigs should pursue any openings and vacancies that interest him and also not hesitate to bring their talents and skills to the attention of others. Those seeking work should actively pursue any openings that they see and, while there may be some disappointments in their quest for work, provided they remain persistent they will find their efforts rewarded. They could also find that once they have obtained a position, this will lead to better opportunities in the future. The early and closing months of the year will be particularly active and favourable times for career matters. All Pigs will also benefit from any courses that they can go on which would widen their skills and experience. The year holds a lot of potential for the Pig and by adopting a positive and determined attitude, he can make considerable progress and receive due recognition for his many talents.

Financial matters are also well aspected and the Pig will enjoy an improvement in his financial situation over the year. He could also be most fortunate in some purchases that he makes – particularly personal items, such as clothes, as well as items for his home – and by keeping alert he could spot some bargains in the most unlikely of places! Providing he does not take unnecessary risks, investments or a savings policy that he takes out could prove most rewarding for him.

The Pig will also gain much over the year from personal study and, if there has been a subject that has been intriguing him, now would be a good time to find out more. Those Pigs involved in education will find that their studies go well and their results will more than justify any sacrifices in time and energy they have had to make.

The Pig will enjoy the travelling that he undertakes over the year and the journeys, holidays and breaks are all likely to go well. He could also get much pleasure from outdoor activities and for those Pigs who enjoy gardening, exploring the countryside or who follow sport, the year is likely to contain many satisfying moments.

On a personal level, this will be a happy and memorable year for the Pig. His family will give him much valuable support for his various activities and he will also take great delight in the achievement and successes enjoyed by some of those around him. Many Pigs could see an addition to their family over the year or have some other good reason for a major family celebration. They can also look forward to an active social life and will attend some enjoyable parties and functions over the year. For the unattached Pig, romance is most favourably aspected and many could meet their future partner over the year, get engaged or married.

However, while 1995 will be a successful and generally happy year for the Pig, he should not neglect his own well-being. He would do well to make sure that he eats a well-balanced diet and takes regular exercise. Also, with his great capacity for enjoying himself, the Pig is sometimes tempted to overdo things and 'burn the candle at both ends'. Without care, he could become tired and leave himself prone to colds and other minor ailments. The Pig can have a lot of fun in 1995, but it would be best if this fun were not at the expense of his own well-being!

Generally, however, 1995 will be an excellent year for the Pig. His domestic and social life will give him much happiness and there will be plenty of opportunities for him to make progress in his career. This is the Year of the Pig and for those Pigs who are prepared to go after their objectives, no matter what they are, the year could be one of the most successful and rewarding they have enjoyed for a long time.

As far as the different types of Pig are concerned, 1995 will be an interesting and rewarding year for the *Metal Pig*. Over the year several important changes will take place and these will open up new and brighter opportunities for him. He is likely to change his work or take on new responsibilities, and his new duties will give him a better chance to demonstrate his many skills and talents. Throughout the year he should certainly pursue any openings that he sees and also take advantage of any opportunity he gets to widen his experience. With a positive attitude, he can accomplish much in 1995. February, March and October are likely to be particularly favourable months for career matters. The Metal Pig will also see an improvement in his finances over the year although it would be in his interests to keep a watchful eye over his general level of expenditure. Without care, this could easily exceed his income and result in problems later. Personally, this will be a very happy year and he will be much in demand with his family and friends. In particular, a dear and close relation will be a great source of pride and happiness to him and will give him much valuable encouragement and advice as the year progresses. For those Metal Pigs who are unattached there will be many opportunities to make new friends and romance is very favourably aspected. From a personal point of view, 1995 will be one of the happiest years that the Metal Pig has enjoyed for some time and if there has been some adversity in his life in recent times, he would do well to view 1995 as the start of a new and improved phase in his life. The year will see several significant and positive changes taking place and the Metal Pig will emerge from it with some worthy gains to his credit.

This will be a most pleasurable year for the *Water Pig*. In 1995 he will be able to devote much time to his family and interests and both will be a great source of pleasure for him. He will also attend some most enjoyable social occasions over the year and many Water Pigs can look forward to leading a busier social life than they may have had in recent times. If the Water Pig finds he has some spare time at his disposal he would do well to consider taking up a new interest, preferably one which would enable him to use his creative talents. He could find writing, drawing, music or photography especially enjoyable. Similarly, if he feels in need of some additional company, he should consider joining a local group or society. Anything positive that he can do over the year will bring pleasing results. Financially, this will also be a favourable year and many Water Pigs can look forward to some pleasing financial news during the summer. However, despite any financial good fortune he might enjoy, the Water Pig should avoid becoming complacent in financial matters and particularly resist being persuaded into any transaction against his better judgement. He would also do well to check the terms of any large transaction he enters into over the year. Provided he is cautious and prudent, his financial situation will improve substantially over the year. There will be several opportunities for the Water Pig to travel during the year and any breaks and holidays that he takes are likely to prove enjoyable and beneficial for him. He should also take advantage of any opportunity that he gets to visit friends or relations that he has not seen for some time. Generally, 1995 will be a very satisfying year for him and provided he uses his time constructively and sets about his activities in a positive frame of mind, he will obtain some pleasing and worthwhile results.

This will be a memorable and satisfying year for the *Wood Pig*. Over the last year he is likely to have given much thought to his present situation and future and 1995 will be an ideal year to put any plans he has into action. These could concern his accommodation, travel, his career or achieving a personal ambition, but whatever his ideas are, by acting decisively he will get results. This is very much a year of action and almost all that the Wood Pig undertakes will work out in his favour. He will also receive valuable support from his family and friends and should he have any worries or be in a dilemma over any matter during the year, he should not hesitate to seek advice. Help and encouragement are there, should he require them. Financially, this will also be a most successful year for him and many Wood Pigs will receive an additional and welcome sum of money. Provided he does not fritter any spare money away needlessly, the Wood Pig's financial situation will improve considerably and some savings or investments he makes could prove most useful to him in the future. His social and domestic life will give him much pleasure and he can look forward to some very happy times with his family and friends. Although some parts of the year will be busy, there will be others when he can devote time to his hobbies and interests and these are likely to bring him much satisfaction. If he does not have a hobby he can turn to at a spare moment, he would do well to take one up. All Wood Pigs will find that by using their time constructively, they will achieve satisfying results as well as enjoying the year. The Wood Pig will also thoroughly enjoy any journeys that he takes in 1995, particularly to places he has not visited before.

This can be an excellent and fulfilling year for the *Fire Pig*, although the amount of success he enjoys is heavily dependent upon his attitude. The Fire Pig has many talents but does not always enjoy as much success as he could. Sometimes he squanders his energies by involving himself in more things that he can sensibly handle, or gets so wrapped up in his own concerns that he does not take as much notice of the views of others as he should. In 1995 he needs to concentrate on specific objectives and involve others in his activities; if he can do this he can accomplish much. He will also greatly benefit from the advice and support he is given over the year. There will be plenty of opportunities for the Fire Pig to pursue in his work and if he is dissatisfied with his present position or is seeking employment, he should actively pursue any openings that he sees. Many Fire Pigs will change the nature of their duties over the year and while they might find this change daunting at first, they will be stimulated by the challenge that it brings. This will also be a favourable year for financial matters and if the Fire Pig has any spare money over the year he would do well to consider putting some funds aside for a specific purpose or investing them for the future. The one thing he should avoid is frittering away any surplus money on needless extravagances. Without a certain restraint, any financial good fortune he enjoys could be short-lived! The Fire Pig's domestic life will be busy and enjoyable and he is likely to spend much time over the year in carrying out improvements and modifications to his home. The work he carries out will give both him and those around him much satisfaction. He will also lead a pleasant social life in 1995 and any travelling he undertakes will go well.

This will be a very positive and satisfying year for the *Earth Pig*. He can look forward to making considerable progress in his work, with new and brighter opportunities appearing as the year develops. However, to maximize the favourable trends that exist, the Earth Pig needs to be relatively flexible in his attitude and adapt to changing situations. By doing this and continuing to act in his usual positive and conscientious way, he can do extremely well. This is a year of considerable opportunity and it rests with him to go after his objectives and make the most of his many talents. Similarly, if the Earth Pig is seeking employment or is unhappy in his present position, he should make a determined effort to follow up any openings that he sees. This year can represent a new and positive phase in the Earth Pig's life and many of his accomplishments now will help to set the pattern for future years as well. In addition to the positive aspects in his work, the Earth Pig will also do well in financial matters and will enjoy a noticeable improvement in his financial situation over the year. He can look forward to some very happy times with his family and friends and throughout the year he would do well to involve those around him in his various activities. He will also delight in the achievements and successes enjoyed by a close relation and any additional support that the Earth Pig can give will be much appreciated. There will also be opportunities for him to travel over the year and any holidays he takes are likely to be most enjoyable and beneficial. Generally, 1995 will be an excellent year for the Earth Pig and provided he is prepared to be flexible in his outlook and adjust to changes as they occur, he will do very well over the year and make considerable progress.

FAMOUS PIGS

Russ Abbot, Bryan Adams, Woody Allen, Julie Andrews, Fred Astaire, Sir Richard Attenborough, Jeremy Beadle, Gerhard Berger, Hector Berlioz, David Blunkett, Humphrey Bogart, Maria Callas, Dr George Carey, Richard Chamberlain, Hillary Clinton, Glenn Close, Brian Clough, Sir Noël Coward, Oliver Cromwell, the Dalai Lama, Sir Robin Day, Richard Dreyfuss, Sheena Easton, Ralph Waldo Emerson, David Essex, Farrah Fawcett, Henry Ford, Debbie Greenwood, Emmylou Harris, Chesney Hawkes, William Randolph Hearst, Ernest Hemingway, Henry VIII, Alfred Hitchcock, King Hussein of Jordan, Elton John, C. G. Jung, Boris Karloff, Stephen King, Nastassja Kinski, Henry Kissinger, Kevin Kline, Jerry Lee Lewis, John McEnroe, Marcel Marceau, Johnny Mathis, Montgomery of Alamein, Dudley Moore, Patrick Moore, John Mortimer, Wolfgang Amadeus Mozart, Olivia Newton John, Michael Parkinson, Luciano Pavarotti, Lester Piggott, Maurice Ravel, Dan Quayle, Ronald Reagan, Albert Reynolds, John D. Rockefeller, Ginger Rogers, Nick Ross, Sade, Salman Rushdie, Baroness Sue Ryder of Warsaw, Pete Sampras, Arnold Schwarzenegger, Albert Schweitzer, Donald Sinden, Steven Spielberg, Emma Thompson, Tracey Ullman, the Duchess of York.

APPENDIX

The relationship between the 12 animal signs – both on a personal level and business level – is an important aspect of Chinese horoscopes and in this Appendix the compatibility between the signs is shown in the two tables that follow. Also included are the names of the signs ruling the hours of the day and from this it is possible to find your ascendant and discover yet another aspect of your personality.

PERSONAL RELATIONSHIPS

KEY
1 Excellent. Great rapport.
2 A successful relationship. Many interests in common.
3 Mutual respect and understanding. A good relationship.
4 Fair. Needs care and some willingness to compromise in order for the relationship to work.
5 Awkward. Possible difficulties in communication with few interests in common.
6 A clash of personalities. Very difficult.

	Rat	Ox	Tiger	Rabbit	Dragon	Snake	Horse	Goat	Monkey	Rooster	Dog	Pig
Rat	1											
Ox	1	3										
Tiger	4	6	5									
Rabbit	5	2	3	3								
Dragon	1	5	5	3	2							
Snake	3	1	6	2	1	5						
Horse	6	5	1	4	3	4	2					
Goat	5	5	3	1	4	3	2	2				
Monkey	1	3	6	3	1	3	5	3	1			
Rooster	4	1	4	6	2	1	2	4	5	5		
Dog	3	4	1	3	6	3	2	5	3	5	2	
Pig	2	3	2	2	3	6	3	2	2	3	1	2

BUSINESS RELATIONSHIPS

KEY
1 Excellent. Marvellous understanding and rapport.
2 Very good. Complement each other well.
3 A good working relationship and understanding can be developed.
4 Fair, but compromise and a common objective is often needed to make this relationship work.
5 Awkward. Unlikely to work, either through lack of trust, understanding or the competitiveness of the signs.
6 Mistrust. Difficult. To be avoided.

	Rat	Ox	Tiger	Rabbit	Dragon	Snake	Horse	Goat	Monkey	Rooster	Dog	Pig
Rat	2											
Ox	1	3										
Tiger	3	6	5									
Rabbit	4	3	4	3								
Dragon	1	4	3	4	3							
Snake	3	2	6	4	1	5						
Horse	6	4	1	4	3	4	3					
Goat	4	5	3	1	4	3	3	2				
Monkey	2	3	4	5	1	5	4	4	3			
Rooster	5	1	5	5	2	1	2	5	4	6		
Dog	4	5	2	3	6	3	2	5	3	5	3	
Pig	3	3	2	2	4	5	4	2	3	4	3	3

YOUR ASCENDANT

The ascendant has a very strong influence on your personality and, together with the information already given about your sign and the effects of the element on your sign, it will help you gain even greater insight into your true personality according to Chinese horoscopes.

The hours of the day are named after the 12 animal signs and the sign governing the time you were born is your ascendant. To find your ascendant, look up the time of your birth on the table below, bearing in mind any local time differences in the place you were born.

11 p.m.	to	1 a.m.	The hours of the Rat
1 a.m.	to	3 a.m.	The hours of the Ox
3 a.m.	to	5 a.m.	The hours of the Tiger
5 a.m.	to	7 a.m.	The hours of the Rabbit
7 a.m.	to	9 a.m.	The hours of the Dragon
9 a.m.	to	11 a.m.	The hours of the Snake
11 a.m.	to	1 p.m.	The hours of the Horse
1 p.m.	to	3 p.m.	The hours of the Goat
3 p.m.	to	5 p.m.	The hours of the Monkey
5 p.m.	to	7 p.m.	The hours of the Rooster
7 p.m.	to	9 p.m.	The hours of the Dog
9 p.m.	to	11 p.m.	The hours of the Pig

RAT: The influence of the Rat as ascendant is likely to make the sign more outgoing, sociable and also more careful with money. A particularly beneficial influence for those born under the sign of the Rabbit, Horse, Monkey and Pig.

OX: The Ox as ascendant has a restraining, cautionary and steadying influence which many signs will benefit from. This ascendant also promotes self-confidence and will-power and is an especially good ascendant for those born under the signs of the Tiger, Rabbit and Goat.

TIGER: This ascendant is a dynamic and stirring influence which makes the sign more outgoing, more action-orientated and more impulsive. A generally favourable ascendant for the Ox, Tiger, Snake and Horse.

RABBIT: The Rabbit as ascendant has a moderating influence, making the sign more reflective, serene and discreet. A particularly beneficial influence for the Rat, Dragon, Monkey and Rooster.

DRAGON: The Dragon as ascendant gives strength, determination and an added ambition to the sign. A favourable influence for those born under the signs of the Rabbit, Goat, Monkey and Dog.

SNAKE: The Snake as ascendant can make the sign more reflective, more intuitive and more self-reliant. A good influence for the Tiger, Goat and Pig.

HORSE: The influence of the Horse will make the sign more adventurous, more daring and, on some occasions, more fickle. Generally a beneficial influence for the Rabbit, Snake, Dog and Pig.

GOAT: This ascendant will make the sign more tolerant, easy-going and receptive. The Goat could also impart some creative and artistic qualities to the sign. An especially good influence for the Ox, Dragon, Snake and Rooster.

MONKEY: The Monkey as ascendant is likely to impart a delicious sense of humour and fun to the sign. He will make the sign more enterprising and outgoing – a particularly good influence for the Rat, Ox, Snake and Goat.

ROOSTER: The Rooster as ascendant helps to give the sign a lively, outgoing and very methodical manner. Its influence will increase efficiency and is a good influence for the Ox, Tiger, Rabbit and Horse.

DOG: The Dog as ascendant makes the sign more reasonable and fair-minded as well as giving an added sense of loyalty. A very good ascendant for the Tiger, Dragon and Goat.

PIG: The influence of the Pig can make the sign more sociable, content and self-indulgent. It is also a caring influence and one which can make the sign want to help others. A good ascendant for the Dragon and Monkey.

HOW TO GET THE BEST FROM THE YEAR

One of the chief values of Chinese horoscopes is that they help to identify trends for the forthcoming year. Once these trends have been identified, it is possible for each sign to know what areas of life are likely to proceed well and which could prove more troublesome. With this knowledge, the more favourably aspected areas can be concentrated on and care can be taken in those areas where the aspects are not so favourable. In this respect, Chinese horoscopes can serve as a useful guide.

Here, to supplement the earlier sections on the prospects for each of the signs, I have indicated how I believe each will fare in 1995 and how each can get the best from the year. The areas covered are: general prospects, finance, career prospects and relations with others.

General Prospects

RAT: This will be a generally positive year for the Rat and his accomplishments will go a long way towards preparing him for his future successes, particularly for those in his own year, 1996. Throughout 1995, however, he should actively pursue any opportunities that he sees, widen his experience and also give some thought to his future objectives. In many of his activities the Rat would do well to join forces with others rather than retain too independent an attitude.

OX: A positive and fulfilling year ahead. Many Oxen will see several changes taking place in their life and out of these will emerge new and brighter opportunities. This is a year for the Ox to pursue his ambitions and if, in recent times, he has felt he has been in a rut or has been dissatisfied with his progress, 1995 is the year to take positive action. For the determined Ox, this can be a successful and rewarding year.

TIGER: An enjoyable and constructive year. This is very much an action-orientated year for the Tiger and by pursuing his objectives, the Tiger can accomplish a great deal in many areas of his life. This is a year of positive change and a time for the Tiger to be bold and determined to make the most of his many capabilities.

RABBIT: This will be a satisfying and pleasant year for the Rabbit. He will make steady progress in many of his activities but his greatest pleasure will come from his family and friends. Romance is especially well aspected.

DRAGON: The Dragon has many talents and he can put these to good use over the year. This is a time for him actively to pursue his ambitions and to be his bold and enterprising self! He can make good progress over the year. Property matters do need careful handling, but travel is well aspected.

SNAKE: A challenging year. The Snake should be cautious in his various activities and remain alert and watchful to all that is going on around him. He should also give much thought to his future. The experience he gains and plans he makes in 1995 will prove very significant in the next few years.

HORSE: A reasonable year; while the Horse will make progress, he could experience problems and delays with some of his activities. He will do best by concentrating on specific matters and not taking on too much all at the same time. As the year will be quite demanding, he should also make sure he does not neglect his own well-being and devotes time to any of his interests that would help him to rest and unwind.

GOAT: A favourable year ahead. The Goat should set about his activities with renewed determination and if he has any objective he wishes to achieve or wants to improve upon his present position, then he should act. The bold and determined Goat will accomplish much over the year.

MONKEY: A reasonably good year but the Monkey should plan his activities carefully and avoid taking unnecessary risks. He would do well to set himself some objectives to aim for and concentrate on these rather than spread his energies too widely. With a careful and positive approach he can accomplish much in 1995, but legal matters and important paperwork do need careful handling.

ROOSTER: A year of considerable opportunities. However, the Rooster should have some idea of what he wants to achieve over the year and go after his objectives in his usual determined and methodical manner. The year will contain many happy times for him although accommodation and property matters do need careful handling.

DOG: A busy but fulfilling year. The Dog should continue to set about his activities in his usual conscientious way and pursue any opportunities that he sees. He can make good and constructive progress. Travel plans do need careful attention but generally, despite the demanding nature of the year, 1995 will still contain many happy times for him.

PIG: A super year ahead. However, the Pig needs to give some thought to what he wishes to achieve over the year and work purposefully towards his objectives. This will be a year of great progress and by giving of his best, the Pig can achieve a great deal. Positive and determined action will bring results.

Finance

RAT: Although the Rat is usually careful in financial matters, he can sometimes be indulgent and extravagant in his personal spending. In 1995 he should keep a careful watch on his level of expenditure and not take any unnecessary risks with his money. This is a year for care and prudence.

OX: A highly favourable year for financial matters.

TIGER: The Tiger should avoid risky ventures and keep a close watch over his level of spending. This is a year for prudence and restraint.

RABBIT: Although the Rabbit is usually very adept when dealing with financial matters, care is needed in 1995. He would do well to avoid entering into risky undertakings and should also keep a close watch on his general level of outgoings. The Rabbit should also check the details and terms of any large transaction he enters into over the year. This is not a time when he can afford to be complacent or careless in money matters.

DRAGON: The Dragon will see an upturn in his financial situation over the year and could be successful in some investments he makes.

SNAKE: The Snake can be highly successful in financial matters in 1995 provided he does not take unnecessary risks with his money.

HORSE: Many Horses will see a noticeable upturn in financial matters over the year. Transactions concerning property do, however, need careful handling.

GOAT: A generally good year for financial matters although, with his sometimes rather indulgent nature, the Goat would do well to keep a watch on his general level of spending. However, he could be fortunate in making several worthwhile acquisitions over the year, particularly items for his home.

MONKEY: A generally good year for financial matters, although the Monkey should not take unnecessary risks or become complacent in money matters. If he is careful and prudent, he will see a steady improvement in his finances.

ROOSTER: A good year for financial matters, although the Rooster should be wary about spending large amounts on the spur of the moment.

DOG: A good year for financial matters. If the Dog is able to make any savings for his long-term future he could find these will develop into a useful asset in years to come.

PIG: A favourable year for financial matters, although it would still be in the Pig's interests to remain prudent in his financial dealings. Sometimes he can be a little too carefree in his spending and any surplus he has built up could quickly evaporate. With care, caution and restraint, however, his financial situation will greatly improve over the year.

Career Prospects

RAT: The Rat can make significant progress in his career and many Rats will move to a better and more rewarding position. The Rat should pursue any opportunities that he sees and try to widen his skills and experience. His accomplishments during 1995 will help to pave the way for even greater progress next year. This is a year to remain positive and determined.

OX: This will be a year of considerable opportunity for the Ox. He should remain alert to all that is going on around him and follow up any openings that he sees. Changes that take place over the year can bring some excellent opportunities for him. He should also seize any chance he has to extend his experience and skills.

TIGER: Great progress is possible. The Tiger should advance his ideas and pursue any openings and opportunities he sees. Even if his initial efforts fail, he should remain persistent and undaunted. With a determined attitude, he can do very well in work matters and many Tigers will be successful in gaining a new and better position over the year.

RABBIT: The Rabbit can make reasonably good progress over the year, particularly if his work is of a creative nature. However, he would do well to make sure that he has the backing of others before carrying out new plans and avoid taking unnecessary career risks. By proceeding carefully and in his usual conscientious way, the Rabbit can do well. Many will take on new duties and responsibilities as the year progresses.

DRAGON: The Dragon can make substantial progress over the year. If he is able to widen his experience he will find this will do much to help his future prospects. He should also advance any ideas he has. This year will hold many positive opportunities for the Dragon.

SNAKE: The Snake should continue to set about his work in his usual conscientious manner and follow up any opportunities that he sees. He should avoid taking risks or trying to accomplish too much too soon. He would also do well to widen his experience over the year.

HORSE: A year of positive progress and interesting new challenges.

GOAT: The Goat can do very well in his career over the year. He should actively follow up any opportunities that he sees and promote himself and his skills. Many Goats will be successful in gaining new responsibilities and a better position in 1995.

MONKEY: Good progress is possible. However, the Monkey does need to work closely with others and pay careful attention to all that is going on around him. Although he likes to be his own master, 1995 is not a year when he can rely just on his own efforts. He should pursue the opportunities that he sees and would also do well to give some thought to his longer-term future.

ROOSTER: A year of pleasing progress. There will be opportunities for new positions or promotion and most Roosters will be able to usefully widen their skills and experience over the year. The Rooster should actively follow up any opportunities that he sees and with a positive and determined attitude he can do extremely well.

DOG: A year of considerable potential. The Dog should pursue any openings that he sees and use any opportunity that he gets to extend his skills and experience. This will be a year of change and progress.

PIG: Great progress is possible, but the Pig needs to push himself forward, promote his talents and ideas and go after the opportunities that he sees. By acting boldly and determinedly, he can do very well in work matters.

Relations with Others

RAT: Socially, this will be a good year, with opportunities for new friends and romance well aspected. However, throughout 1995 the Rat needs to pay careful attention to the views of others and make sure that he has the necessary support before starting any new enterprise.

OX: Romantically and socially, this will be a favourable year. However the Ox will need to deal with family and domestic matters with care and remain mindful of the views of those around them. Where possible, he should encourage joint family interests and make sure he devotes time and attention to his loved ones.

TIGER: While his family and friends will give him much happiness and support over the year, the Tiger still needs to exercise care in his relations with others. He should involve those around him in his activities and if problems – particularly domestic – arise, he should deal with them as they occur rather than let them linger in the background and possibly sour relations unnecessarily. There will be opportunities for new friendships over the year, but the unattached Tiger would do well to let any new romance develop gradually rather than rush into any commitment.

RABBIT: The Rabbit gets on very well with others and 1995 will be no exception to this. His domestic and social life will give him great pleasure and socially this will be a busy and eventful year for him. Many Rabbits who are unattached will fall in love, get engaged or married over the year.

DRAGON: Both domestically and socially the year will contain some happy times. There will be opportunities for new friendships and romance, but romantic matters do need careful handling. Also, the Dragon could find himself in a disagreement with someone over the year and it would be in his interests to resolve the problem as quickly and amicably as he can. Mostly, his relations with others will go well and bring him much happiness, but care is needed!

SNAKE: The Snake's relations with others will go reasonably well over the year although he should remain mindful of the views and interests of those around him and involve others in his various activities. His social life will be pleasurable with plenty of opportunities for romance.

HORSE: The Horse's domestic and social life will bring him much pleasure in 1995 and he would do well to bear in mind any advice that relatives and friends give him over the year. They will always speak with his best interests at heart. Romantic matters are well aspected.

GOAT: Domestically and socially, this will be a happy and enjoyable year. Those around the Goat will be most supportive and he should not hesitate to seek their views if any matter is troubling him. A good year for personal relationships.

MONKEY: Domestically and socially, this will be an active and generally happy year for the Monkey. However, to preserve friendships and domestic harmony, he needs to pay careful attention to the interests and views of those around him. Although there are many who love and admire the Monkey, he must remember that he cannot expect to have everything his own way!

ROOSTER: This will be a happy and enjoyable year both domestically and socially. However, throughout the year the Rooster should be prepared to work closely with others and pay careful attention to all that is going on around him. To become too occupied with his own concerns could cause problems. A favourable year for romance.

DOG: An active time domestically and socially. The Dog's family and friends will give him much pleasure and he can look forward to many happy times with them. If he has any problems or feels under any pressure he should not